Scientific Methods To TOP Every EXAM Of Life

Biswaroop Roy Chowdhury

The only person on earth to hold both mind and body world records.

DIAMOND BOOKS

Resource and reference to create this book :
Bhagvad Geeta, Bible, lives of Mahatma Gandhi, Sachin Tendulkar, Swami Vivekananda, Jagdish Chandra Bose, Einstein, Lance Armstrong, Bruce Lee, Arnold Schwarzenegger, Bhagwan Gautam Buddha and findings of NASA.

The reference is also taken from the works of Dale Carnegie, Anthony Robbins, Napolian Hill, O.P. Bam, Paul Mckenna, LynneMc Taggart and Vincent M. Roazzi.

Author: Biswaroop Roy Chowdhury

Co-authors: Tanu Vashistha
Dr Roop Singh
Rajrup Fuliya
BK Chandra Shekhar
Neerja Roy Chowdhury

Proof reader: Ranjana Monga

Graphics Designer: Shankar Singh Koranga

Design Studio:
Dynamic Memory Pvt. Ltd.
B-121, 2nd Floor, Green Fields
Faridabad-121003
Ph.: 0129-2510534
Website: www.biswaroop.com

ISBN : 978-81-288-3246-8

Published by
Diamond Pocket Books Pvt. Ltd.
X-30, Okhla Industrial Area, Phase-II
New Delhi-110020
Phone : 011-40712200
E-mail : sales@dpb.in
Website : www.diamondbook.in

Scientific Methods to Top Every Exam of Life
By*: Biswaroop Roy Chowdhury*

DEDICATION

Dedicated to my parents
who have been the source of
inspiration for my creative writing.

CONTENTS

Relationship

Mind Body Medicine

Sports

Experiments

Mind Power

Experiments

Academic

Experiments

21 Days Brain Rewiring Master Plan

RELATIONSHIP

EXPERIMENT -1

MIND STICK-I

Can you believe that a stick has an ability to think and we too can read its mind?
Does this surprise you?

Activity I-
Let's experiment with the stick.

Step I –Hold the stick as shown.

Step II- Look at the 'negative' mark on the stick and try to balance it.

Step III-Focus only at the point of the negative mark.

Expected Result :
You will not be able to balance the stick for more than 15 seconds.

Activity II-
Balance the stick once again on your palm looking at the 'positive' mark above.

Expected Result:
You will be able to balance it for a longer period now.

EXPERIMENT -2

MIND STICK II

What do you learn from the Mind Stick Experiment?

1. **Change your focus. Change the result-**
   Same action will not give different results. A new and innovative action will bring about the desired result.
2. **Think positive and have control over your goals-**
   It is not possible to balance your life or achieve your goals by negative thinking. Believe in yourself and have faith that one day your dreams will become a reality.
3. **Not just hard work but smart work is the key to success-** You might try to balance the stick by looking at the bottom but it is difficult. Just by discovering a smarter way to balance (i.e. by changing the focus) you get the desired results immediately.
4. **Anything that seems impossible initially can become simpler later-**
   The task of balancing the stick by looking at the bottom appears impossible but the same task becomes possible and looks simple - just by doing it differently.
5. **Small steps everyday may make a big difference later-**

   Do you wonder - why we were not able to balance the stick initially while looking at the bottom of the stick? The movement at the bottom is not noticeable. By the time we change the position of the palm, it gets too late.

   However when we look at the top of the stick, the small displacement at the bottom gets magnified and we clearly know how to reposition the palm to maintain balance.

   Similarly, when we are learning something the new progress made each day might seem insignificant initially. But remember, drops of water fill an ocean. After sometime, your efforts are sure to bear fruits and show results.

EXPERIMENT -3

PERSONAL MUSEUM FOR BARKING BOSS OR A SHOUTING TEACHER

You mentally rerun that experience the rest of the day, picturing him or her yelling at you over and over again, then you feel progressively worse. Why let the experience continue to affect you? Why not just take this record in your mind and scratch it so many times that you can't experience those feelings anymore? Maybe you can even make it funny.

Now scramble the disempowering feelings until they no longer come up. After reading this, take the following steps.

1) See the situation in your mind that's been bothering you so much. Try to see everything that happened.

2) Take that same experience and turn it into a cartoon. Sit upright in your chair with a big, silly grin on your face, breathing fully, and run the image backward as fast as you can so that you can see everything moving in reverse. If somebody said something, watch them swallow their words. Let the movie run backward in a very fast motion, then run it forward again in an even faster motion. Now change the colors of the images, so that everybody's faces are rainbow-colored. If there's someone in particular who upsets you, then imagine his ears have grown in size like those of Mickey Mouse or the nose has grown like Pinocchio's.

3) Now think about the situation that was bothering you, and notice how you feel now. If done effectively, you would have broken the pattern so many times that you would have easily broken into those negative feelings.

   This can be done with things that have been bothering you for years. It's often a much more effective approach than trying to analyze the 'whys and wherefores' of a situation which doesn't change the sensations you link with the situation.

   As simple as it seems, effectively scrambling a situation will work in most cases, even where trauma has been involved.

Why does it work?

Because our feelings are based on the images we focus on in our minds and the sounds and sensations we link to those specific images. As we change the images and sounds, we change the way we feel. Conditioning this again and again makes it difficult to get back into the old pattern.

EXPERIMENT-4

SCIENCE OF HAPPINESS

Happiness is all about making a decision. Think about it. If you make a million dollars, the million dollars alone won't give you any pleasure. It's a rule and it says, "When I hit this mark, then I'll give myself permission to feel good." At that moment, when you decide to feel good, you send a message to your brain to change its responses to the muscles of your face, chest, and body. To change your breathing and to change the biochemistry within your nervous system that causes you to feel the sensations you call pleasure.

Adopting this rule would raise your standards. It means you would hold yourself to a higher standard of enjoying yourself despite the conditions of the moment. It means you've committed to intelligent evaluations in a way that allows you to experience the true richness of life- maybe that's the ultimate rule.

To ensure the absolute attainment of your goals, you must condition your nervous system in advance to feel the pleasure they will surely bring. In other words, you must rehearse and emotionally enjoy the experience of achieving each one of your most valued goals at least twice a day. Each time you do this, you need to create more emotional joy as you see, feel, and hear yourself living your dream.

This continuous focus will create a neural pathway between where you are and where you want to be. Because of this intense conditioning you'll find yourself feeling a sense of absolute certainty that you'll achieve your desires, and this certainty will translate into a quality of action that ensures your success. Your confidence will allow you to attract the appropriate coaches and role models who will guide you in take the most effective actions to produce results quickly rather than the traditional trial – and –error method that can take decades or more . Don't wait for another day to begin this process. Start Today!

EXPERIMENT-5

SCIENTIFIC BASIS OF FORGIVENESS

Forgiving is necessary. However if you forgive than you might be branded as a coward but now you will know that not forgiving is definitely injurious to your health.

Go to recent past and try to identify a person whom you consider your enemy and who has done a great amount of damage to your life. Think of some relevant moment. Now try to run that mental movie and try to hear each and every word said by that enemy to degrade you.

Now see how do you feel - Tick one of the following.
(a) I feel nothing.
(b) I feel bad.
(c) I feel happy.

Definitely you must be feeling bad and must have felt worse at the moment when it happened as a result you have decided not to forgive that person and take revenge.

Remember, the moment you decide to take revenge will make the mental pain even more intact and biologically it is known that continuous mental pain gets translated into its physical equivalent and gets distributed to our cells, tissues and various other organs of the body which lead to a far greater damage.

So beware that any kind of revenge or thought of revenge itself may trigger a beginning of the physical decay of your most valuable possession, that is your own body.

EXPERIMENT-6

RUBBER BAND METHOD TO OVERCOME BAD HABITS

We all suffer from one or the other kind of mild bad habits like nail-biting, being short tempered, eating too many chocolates or ice cream.

Associating some form of physical pain with these can help you get rid of these habits.

Use the rubber band method to condition your mind to focus solely on the most positive elements in your life.

Step I : Place a rubber band around your wrist.

Step II : Each time a negative, energy sapping, thought enters your mind, or you find yourself engaging in the bad habit you want to overcome. Snap the rubber band. Through the power of conditioning, your mind will associate the pain with negative thinking and you will soon posses a strongly positive mindset.

EXPERIMENT -7

WHY HONESTY IS GOOD FOR YOUR PHYSICAL HEALTH

Go to your recent past and think of a moment when you were dishonest with someone.

Now try to visualize the moment, and if possible try to put yourself in that person's place. How he would feel if he comes to know about your dishonesty. Try to imagine everything in color the way it was at that moment.

Now, see how do you feel? Tick one of the following -
(a) I feel nothing.
(b) I feel bad.
(c) I feel happy.

Even if the act of dishonesty is not too serious; you will feel some amount of negativity inside your heart every time you think of it.

Now remember any kind of negativity, feeling of guilt and any uncomfortable emotion lead to creating a particular kind of bio-chemical changes resulting in continuous loss of body energy. This might lead to temporary illness or physical weakness. A regular and persistent negative thought process or feelings may even attract dreaded disease like cancer etc.

EXPERIMENT -8

THE MORNING POWER QUESTIONS

Remember, ask and you shall receive.

If you ask a terrible question, you'll get a terrible answer. Your mental computer is ever ready to serve you and whatever question you give it, it will surely come up with an answer.

Successful people asked better questions, and as a result, they got better answers. They got answers that empowered them to know exactly what to do in a situation to produce the results they desired.

It's not only the questions you ask, but the questions you fail to ask, that shape your destiny.

Our life experiences are based on what we focus on. The following questions are designed to make you to experience more happiness, excitement, pride, gratitude, joy, commitment, and love every day of your life. Remember, quality questions create a quality life.

Come up with two or three answers to all of these questions and feel fully associated. If you have difficulty discovering an answer simply add the word "could". Example: "What could I be most happy about in my life ?"

1. What am I happy about in my life now?
   What about it, that makes me happy? How does that make me feel?
2. What am I excited about in my life now?
   What about it, that makes me excited? How does that make me feel?
3. What am I proud about in my life now?
   What about it, that makes me proud? How does that make me feel?
4. What am I grateful about in my life now?
   What about it, that makes me grateful?
5. What am I enjoying most in my life right now?
   What about it, that I enjoy? How does that make me feel?
6. What am I committed to in my life right now?
   What about it, that makes me committed? How does that make me feel?

EXPERIMENT -9

STRESS BUSTER –MIND CAPSULE

Six Steps for Instant Relief from Stress

Stress reduces our efficiency and badly affects our studies. Next time you are stressed, think of these six points for instant relief:-

1. According to research, worrying makes you tense and nervous and affects the nerves of your stomach. It actually changes the gastric juices of your stomach and often leads to stomach ulcers.

"Those who do not know how to fight worry, die young."

- Dr. Alexis Carrel

2. One of the worst features of 'worry' is that it destroys our ability to concentrate. When we worry, our mind runs haywire and we lose all the power of decision. However, when we force ourselves to face the worst and accept it mentally, then we eliminate all these vague imaginations and put ourselves in a position where we are able to concentrate on our problem.

3. ***Do this*** **:** Analyze the situation fearlessly and honestly and figure out the worst that could happen as a result of failure. After that calmly devote your time and energy in improving upon the worst which you have already accepted mentally.

4. Carefully read the sentence given below :

A man is not hurt so much by what happened, as by his opinion of 'what happened'. Now follow this unique technique to change your opinion and mood instantly. *Action seems to follow feeling, but actually action and feeling go hand in hand and by regulating the action which is under the direct control of our will, we can indirectly regulate the feeling, which is not.*

So, act as if you are happy, speak and walk cheerfully as if you were already cheerful, if possible, even dance for a moment.

Remember the words of Abraham Lincoln;

"Most *folks are about as happy they make up their mind to be*."

5. *I had blues because I had no shoes, until upon the street, I met a man who had no feet*.

   Read this every morning and you will never have worries for the things you do not have.

6. **Visualization technique**: Keep a mental account of the *happier moments* of your life. Next time you are tense, go back to your happier days by visualizing yourself in that moment .Try to feel the pleasant atmosphere and music of appreciation of your happier moment.

We are not what we are, but what we think we are.

So next time you are stressed, just refer to this for instant relief.

EXPERIMENT-10

WINNING FRIENDS MADE EASY -I

Principle: *Smile*

Your smile is a messenger of your good will. Your smile brightens the lives of all those who see it .To someone who has seen a dozen people frowning, scowling or turning their faces away, your smile is like the sun breaking through the clouds. Especially when, that someone is under pressure from his bosses, his customers, his teachers, parents or children, a smile can help him realize that all is not hopeless and that there is joy in the world.

Principle: *Remember that a person's name is the sweetest and the most important sound in any language for that person*

- We should be aware of the magic contained in a name and realize that this single item is wholly and completely owned by the person whom we are dealing with..... and nobody else .
- The name sets the individual apart; it makes him or her unique among all others.
- The information we are imparting or the request we are making gets special importance when we approach the situation with the name of the individual From a waitress to a senior executive using the names will work wonders as we deal with others.

Principle : *Be a good listener. Encourage others to talk about themselves*

- Remember that the people you are talking to are a hundred times more interested in themselves , their own wants and problems .
- A person' s toothache means more to that person than a famine in China which has probably killed a million people. A boil on

one's neck interests him/ her more than forty earthquakes in Africa. Keep that in mind the next time you have a conversation with someone.

Principle: *Don't criticize, condemn or complain*

- Instead of condemning people, let's try to understand them .
- Let's try to figure out why they behave the way they do.
- This is a lot more profitable and intriguing than criticism; and it breeds sympathy, tolerance and kindness. "To know all is to forgive all."

Principle: *Become genuinely interested in other people*

- You can make more friends in two months by being interested in other people than you can in two years by trying to get other people to be interested in you.

People are not interested in you. They are interested in themselves –morning, noon and night. If you want others to like you and develop real friendship and to be of help to others as well as yourself then keep this principle in mind.

Principle : *Be sympathetic towards the other person's ideas and desires*

- Wouldn't you like to have a magic phrase that would stop arguments, eliminate ill feeling, create good will, and make the other person listen attentively?

Yes? All right .

For example:

- "I don't blame you one iota for feeling like this."
- "If I were you, I would undoubtedly feel the way you do. "

An answer like this can soften the most cantankerous discuss .

- You can say that and be 100 percent sincere, because if you were in his place and situation you would feel the same as he does. If you had inherited the same body, temperament and mind and you had had similar environment and experiences then you would be exactly like him in every respect.

EXPERIMENT -11

WINNING FRIENDS MADE EASY -II

Principle: ***The only way to get the best of an argument is to avoid it***

- Listen first- Give your opponents a chance to talk. Let them finish. Do not resist, defend or debate. This only raises barriers. Try to build bridges of understanding. Don't build higher barriers of misunderstanding.
- Look for areas of agreement. When you have heard your opponents , dwell first on the points and areas on which you agree.
- Be honest. Look for areas where you can admit error and say so. Apologize for your mistakes. It will help disarm your opponents and reduce defensiveness.
- When one yells the other should listen – because when two people yell, there is no communication, just noise and bad vibrations.

Principle : ***If you are wrong, admit it quickly and emphatically***

- You will never get into trouble by admitting that you might be wrong.
- That will stop all argument and inspire your opponent to be just as fair and open and broad –minded as you are .
- It will make him want to admit that he ,too might be wrong.

Principle : ***Get the other person to say "yes, yes" immediately***

- While with people, don't begin by discussing the things on which you differ.
- Begin by emphasizing – and keep on emphasizing – the things on which you agree.

- Keep emphasizing, if possible that you both are striving for the same end and that your only difference is that of the method and not of the purpose. It gets the other person saying "Yes, Yes "at the outset.

Principle : *Try to see things honestly from the other person's point of view*

Remember that other people may be totally wrong. But they don't think so. Don't condemn them. Any fool can do that. Try to understand them.

There is a reason why the other man thinks and acts as he does. Find out that reason and you have the key to his actions, perhaps to his personality. Try honestly to put yourself in his place. If you say to yourself, "How would I Feel, how would I react if I were in his shoes?" you will save your time and irritation, for "by becoming interested in the cause, we are less likely to dislike the effect." And, in addition, you will sharply increase your skill in human relationship.

Principle : *Give honest and sincere appreciation*

Cease thinking of our accomplishments, our wants. Try to figure out the other person's good points. Then forget flattery. Give honest, sincere appreciation. Be hearty in your approbation and lavish in your praise and people will cherish your words and treasure them and repeat them over a lifetime-repeat them years after you have forgotten them.

Principle : *Let the other person do a great deal to the talking*

Let the other people talk themselves out. They know more about their business and problems than you do. So ask them questions. Let them tell you a few things.

If you disagree with them you may be tempted to interrupt. But don't. It is dangerous. They won't pay attention to you while they still have a lot of ideas of their own crying for expression. So listen patiently and with an open mind. Be sincere about it. Encourage them to express their ideas fully.

EXPERIMENT-12

THE PLANT APPRECIATION EXPERIMENT

Step I: Plant identical seedlings in three different pots with the same amount and type of potting soil in each pot.

Step II: Place the pots side by side, so the three plants receive the similar amount of light. Put same amount of manure and water in each pot.

Step III: The only variance in their treatment would be that you will talk to each plant differently.

a) To the first plant, say only appreciative things, such as, "What a wonderful little sapling you are. Look at how delicate your new leaves are, how strongly your little roots hold onto the earth."

b) To the second, say nothing.

c) To the third, say only mean and unappreciative things, such as, "What a pathetic excuse for a seedling you are? You're disgusting. You're not worth the earth I planted you in."

Over the time, the appreciated plant will grow healthy and strong, the neutral plant will grow fairly well, and the unappreciated plant will be stunted and fare poorly.

Now you would know that power of appreciation not only works on humans but plants as well.

MIND BODY MEDICINE

EXPERIMENT -1

THE ORANGE EXPERIMENT

This experiment will help you to understand the mind-body medicine link

(Read the steps once before you perform)

Step I: Bend the fingers of the right hand as if you are holding an orange in it.

Step II: Close your eyes.

Step III: Imagine that you are peeling that orange with both the hands.

Step IV: Now imagine that you are taking off a segment of that orange and bringing it close to your mouth.

Step V: Open your mouth as if you are ready to eat it.

Step VI: Now mentally squeeze that small part of orange and imagine that its juice on your tongue and then feel it moving further in your mouth.

Now just open your eyes and relax.

How did you feel after doing this exercise?

Didn't you feel the taste of orange in your mouth and also secretion of excess saliva on your tongue?

Remember, thoughts and imaginations are connected to each and every cell, tissues and organs of the body.

That means by altering our thoughts and imagination we can alter the biochemical reactions in our body.

We will use this principle in another experiment of this section.

EXPERIMENT -2

THE LAUGHTER CHALLENGE (AN AGE OLD THERAPY)

What happens when we laugh -

1. Hearty laughter helps to regulate the blood pressure.
2. Breathing becomes deeper, which sends oxygen enriched blood and nutrients throughout the body.
3. Laughter decreases the stress hormones.
4. Protects the heart. It helps in preventing heart diseases.
5. Tones intestinal functioning, and strengthens the muscles that hold abdominal organs in place.
6. It can benefit digestion.
7. Hearty laughter can burn calories equivalent to several minutes on the rowing machine or the exercise bike.

8. Laughter stimulates both sides of the brain and this enhances learning. It eases muscle tension and psychological stress, which keeps the brain alert and allows people to retain more information.
9. It increases infection fighting antibodies (antibiotics).
10. It clears negativity, improves attitude and develops overall personality.

In the beginning, you can start out with the artificial laughter, then immediately think of a funny situation of your life that really made you laugh out loud. This will attach itself to your real laughter and make it genuine. In fact "Laughter is a shock absorber that eases the blows of life".

Even artificial laughter will help you reap the same benefits.

EXPERIMENT -3

THE ELECTROMAGNETIC FIELD OF BODY

Our body is a complex electromagnetic field. Our thoughts when converted into images get translated into molecules called neuro-peptides. These have the potential to help us get the thing we imagined or desired with full passion and emotion.

So if you want something (achieving 90% score, in your exams or winning the best athlete award) –

1. Imagine that it has already happened.
2. Visualize the images moving, in color.
3. Feel it, experience it.
4. Visualize it at least 5 times a day. Especially, immediately after waking up and just before going to bed.

This exercise will influence your actions which will lead you to your goal.

EXPERIMENT -4

THE LIFE FORCE OF FOOD

Human beings are the only species on this planet which eats cooked and processed foods.

We are also the only species which regularly suffers from degenerative diseases, and as we are moving more towards heavily cooked and processed diets, the diseases are getting worse.

Along with this, we are also suffering from an array of problems related to lack of energy.

There is one key element in the food which cannot be bottled, manufactured or synthesized. That is the '**life-force**' of food.

Raw foods have their life force intact. This life force can also be preserved by steaming or cooking the food lightly. The common food if cooked at high temperatures, or are heavily processed, they lose their vitality.

Now ask yourself a simple question. How much of what you eat every day is either raw or lightly cooked? Therefore, how much vitality is there in the food you are eating?

Ways to introduce raw foods into your diet

- Eat four pieces of fruit daily for snacks.
- Freshly made juices are the most delightful way to invigorate your life.
- Make a salad with at least ten ingredients: a variety of leaves, a selection of herbs, a large handful of sprouted seeds or grains, any other vegetables like fennel , avocado, olives and anything which can be added to the salad. You can also add some fruit, nuts and seeds to the salad.
- Soups, such as cucumber, tomato, can all be made with very little cooking. Just grind them raw in the blender and then warm them lightly. But be careful about overheating them.
- Use sprouted pulses, beans, seeds, grains and nuts.

EXPERIMENT -5

POWER BREATHING FOR SUPER HEALTH

This technique, will dramatically increase your energy within a couple of weeks of steady use, it is simple to practice and can be done anywhere. It is also one of the best exercises to improve your concentration, if you are weak in this key area.

The Pump

This is a quick energy booster which you may use before a big presentation or an important meeting.

Step I : Simply sit down and place your hands over your belly as if you were cupping a balloon.

Step II: Now pump/push in your stomach at the belly button area and exhale strongly through your nose at the same time.

Step III: Then, inhale through your nose and push the belly outward. Repeat the process twenty times, speeding up as your comfort level goes up.

EXPERIMENT -6

DISCOVER THE SUPERMAN IN YOU

Practice the following daily for just a minute to discover the superman within you.

The superman means a man nurtured with seven values. Seven values are encoded in our supra conscious mind in terms of colors. Visualizing different cosmic colors more than 17 seconds by third eye, triggers emotions of related values and with regular practice the man starts manifesting those values in life and thus discovers the perfect personality within.

Do the following for just a minute frequently or at least hourly or minimum 14 times in a day to get the desired result:-

- Sit comfortably with your eyes closed. Take a few deep breaths and relax.
- Imagine God is showering golden yellow colored rays over your head. Visualize the rays slowly descending through your head until it fills your entire body with joy and happiness. Imagine that this light is cleaning and healing your spirit.
- Practice this frequently until it becomes familiar to you.

Next time repeat this action by visualizing showers of red colored rays. Imagine that the divine healing red rays entering from the top of your head, filling every atom of your body with divine powers and empowering mind and then completely surrounding you. Bask in it. Inwardly say some short phrases such as "I am the superman – the most powerful soul" or "I am radiating divine powers".

Continue slowly through the color spectrum –

1. Orange for purity
2. Green for love
3. Blue for peace
4. Indigo for knowledge
5. Violet for bliss

Until you feel completely perfect and strong.

EXPERIMENT -7

NEUROBICS – THE AEROBICS OF MIND

Neurobics is the best methodology to exercise your mind muscles. Neurobics help you to use your mind power, for creative works. It heals your body and keeps you mentally and physically healthy.

Three pronged strategy of breathing action, hand gestures (*Hasta Mudra*) & visualizing different colors of cosmic light is the key to Neurobics. *To learn the neurobics, it is essential to learn the secret of hand gestures called hasta-mudras.* These hand gestures are very effective if done in the right manner.

1. Hastamudras

After intensive research, Indian sages have found that *Hastamudras* (hand gestures) are very important for keeping a balance in the energy flow between the five elements. *This has tremendous healing power and if practised properly, all major diseases can be cured.*

All five fingers regulate the five elements of body. These are as follows:

- Thumb - Fire element
- Index finger - Air element
- Middle finger - Space or Ether element
- Ring finger - Earth element
- Little finger - Water element

Remember following important points while doing neurobics with various hand Gestures (*Hasta – Mudra*):

- These must be practiced for minimum 15 to 20 minutes at a time.
- For Immediate result, it should be done for 30 to 40 minutes in a day.
- These must be practised with both hands.
- While practising a particular mudra the other fingers must be kept straight.

Now sit in Gyan Mudra, take a long breath and vividly visualize the following to energize your brain and build mind-muscles. If the images don't appear as bright as you want, don't try to force them into being. Instead focus on the idea of seeing an image, know that whatever you are trying to visualize has a shape, a texture, a color, and a size. Take your own time to allow the image to become steady and sharp: -

1 Visualisation of the real things:

A familiar face, A sunset ocean, A childhood friend, A flying eagle, Your bedroom, A drop of dew, A snow capped peak, An ocean & its waves,

2 Visualization of unrealistic things:

A demigod with six arms, A talking giraffe, A chocolate river, A thirty foot ant or visualize five things that are blue, red etc., visualize things beginning with the letter A ....., visualize things that are larger than a bus, visualize things that are found under the ground, visualize things that make you feel happy.

EXPERIMENT -8

THE HOT WATER THERAPY

Drinking hot water is like taking a sauna bath. It purifies the body. How? The reasoning goes like this:-

- As you drink hot water, your body temperature rises slightly.
- To maintain its average 98.6 degrees Fahrenheit, your body begins to perspire. Perspiration has its method of cooling itself.
- Perspiration induced by drinking hot water flushes toxins from your body, helping to purify your bloodstream.
- Additionally, drinking hot water helps remove deposits in the nervous system. These deposits are believed to have a negative effect on thoughts and emotional responses.
- By drinking hot water, you can thus purify mind and body.
- Keeps joints moving, restores and preserves flexibility and strength.
- Protects joints against further damage.
- Manages your weight. Improves coordination. Increases endurance.
- Promotes feelings of well being and self esteem.
- Loosens stiff joints and relieves muscle soreness.

To purify yourself, try drinking hot water daily. The water should be hot enough to make you perspire but should not burn your mouth. You should begin to sweat as your body would try to lower its temperature. When you stop sweating, try drinking hot water again to balance your body temperature.

Nasal Cavity Clearance

Drinking hot water can also be effective in clearing nasal cavities. If you are ill, drinking hot water will make you feel less congested. The water vapors cause the built up in the nasal cavities to loosen.

Why not coffee or tea? Drinking hot water gives you the warmth without dehydrating you which a caffeine drink would.

If drinking plain hot water is unappetizing, you can add a slice of lemon.

EXPERIMENT -9

MIND SNACKS

A Mind Snack means the activities , which can break your routine brain wave pattern.

It involves doing some activities in novel ways to break the brain circuits, balance the brain waves and tone up the neurons. These activities also produce neuro-trophin hormones and make our brain cells healthy. Do the followings whenever you need a break:

1. **Requires participation of one or more** of your senses in a novel way. Here are a few examples:
   - Try to discern the ingredient/source of juices or drinks that you take simply by tasting their flavor.
   - You can also combine two or more senses in unexpected ways, for example, listen to a specific piece of music while smelling a particular aroma or reading a book.
2. **Break your routine in a significant way.** Examples:
   - Take a completely different route to work or school or college.
   - Prepare a breakfast that you don't have normally. Try eating noodles with a spoon instead of a fork.
3. **Explore a new environment:** Go to a new park, garden, mall, theatre, or a new store.
4. **Smell new odors in the morning:** Have new odors, like a bottle of mint extract ready to smell first thing in the morning, to "awaken" your brain. Just after getting out of your bed in the morning, visit your garden or balcony and inhale the fragrance of Roses, Hyacinths, Lillies and Tulips. It flushes in a natural feel-good fragrance.

5. **Perform tasks with your eyes closed:** The other senses become more active and keen once you shut your eyes, since it blocks any distractions. You become more aware of your sub conscious mind. That helps you to recollect important things, the brain usually clears off from the buffer. You can introspect your actions and take decisions as to how would you cope with challenging problems. So you can take a shower, eat or dress yourself up with your eyes closed. Normally you rely on your eyes for these tasks.

6. **Try using your non-dominant hand for performing tasks:** Practice writing, brushing teeth, combing your hair, typing etc with non-dominant hands can teach your brain new things everyday and tear away from the boredom of routine work.

7. **Put on different clothes:** Ever noticed how you feel differently when you wear different clothes? You may think differently as well. It is a scientifically proven fact that different colors generate different vibes and influence your mood's peaks or falls.

8. **Pamper your looks:** Try to wear shades that suit your skin color and dress according to what suits your figure. Give yourself a haircut that will suit your face-cut. No one is asking you to transform into a ramp model, but paying attention to your looks and drawing best out of it, will boost your confidence and lend you a feel-good-factor.

EXPERIMENT -10

MEET THE INVISIBLE DOCTOR – IMMUNOLOGIST

Benefits: This exercise eliminates useless waste thoughts from the mind and also eliminates traces of many hereditary diseases. It makes skin very soft, removes pimples and keeps the body healthy by strengthening its immune system. It also purifies blood, reduces blood pressure and raises defence mechanism of the body.

To reduce blood pressure and raise defence mechanism of body. Take following steps for neurobics:

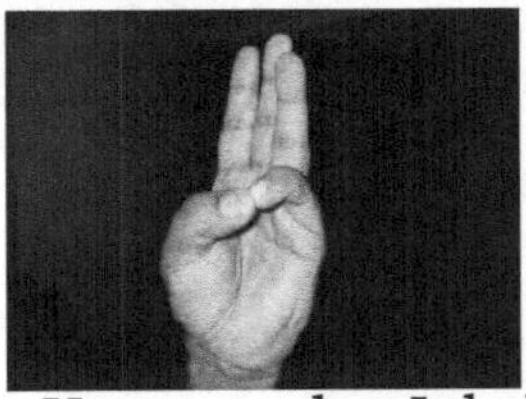

Step – 1: Sit in comfortable position in Varun mudra. Inhale and exhale deeply and slowly five times with both the nostrils. Visualize orange colour while inhaling (feel an orange gas is spreading and purifying all blood cells in the whole body inside) and visualize dark fumes coming out of your nostrils while exhaling (feeling all toxins are coming out).

Step – 2: Close your right nostril with right thumb (left hand in Varun mudra) and inhale and exhale deeply and slowly five times from your left nostril, without making any sound. Also visualize and feel colours as in step – 1.

Step – 3: Now close your left nostril with left thumb (right hand in Varun mudra) and inhale and exhale deeply and slowly five times from your right nostril, without making any sound. Also visualize and feel the colours as in step – 1.

Doing step 1, 2 and 3 completes one cycle. You must do 5 cycles (15 times Breathing in and out) to purify your blood cells.

EXPERIMENT -11

MEET THE INVISIBLE DOCTOR – NEUROLOGIST

Benefits –It helps in getting rid of brain disorders, migraines, nerves and eye disorder. This helps us in stabilizing the mind and the body in the beginning and strengthens the spirit as the final result. We do this with chanting the sound – "O".

The purpose of chanting is to make our mind still and peaceful and take us beyond the realm of super consciousness. Chanting provides emotional excitement and raises psychic power to a very intense level. It is an instant energy booster. *This neurobic enlightens the mind. It opens the third eye and develops creativity.*

"O" is the only vowel, which is the combination of A and U (first and the last vowel). Chanting of "O" creates vibrations in the five elements of the physical body and humming after chanting "O" creates vibrations in "Agya" chakra.

Follow the steps given below: -

Step -1. Sit down comfortably, either cross legged or in the chair. Ensure your back is straight and hands are in 'Pran Mudra' (as shown in the picture).

Step -2. Visualize inhaling indigo (Navy blue) colored gas slowly and deeply.

Step -3. Now curl your lips to make an "O" shape.

Step -4. Breathe out slowly and completely with

"Oooo---" sound while exhaling. Feel all black toxin gases releasing from your body.

Step – 5. Now repeat the above steps for minimum 5 to 10 minutes.

OM or AUM is the most widely chanted phrase across religions and cultures. Some popular chants with Om resonating are Tibetan mantra *Namo Arihantanam Namo Namo* and Sikh mantra *Ek Omkar Satnam* or *Allah-O-Akbar* in Islam. This is the basic trinity of sounds and the whole music of life grows out of this.

EXPERIMENT -12

MEET THE INVISIBLE DOCTOR - ENDOCRINOLOGIST

Benefits:- Doing this blissful sound neurobics creates the frequency of 2000 htz per second in all the cells and tissues of our body, which in turn triggers the production of endorphins and encephalin hormones in the brain, which evoke the feelings of bliss, as well as dulls the perception of pain. This exercise makes our sleep effective and reduces the time of sleep cycles. This exercise also increases memory and mind power to a great extent.

These blissful sounds are called humming sounds. This sound is the combination of M and N sound, which are in the middle of the 26 alphabets. Take the following steps to do this neurobic :

Step – 1: Sit down comfortably either cross-legged or in a chair. Ensure that your back is straight and hands are in 'Dhyan Mudra' (as in the picture).

Step -2 : Fold your tongue and touch the palate and close your mouth.

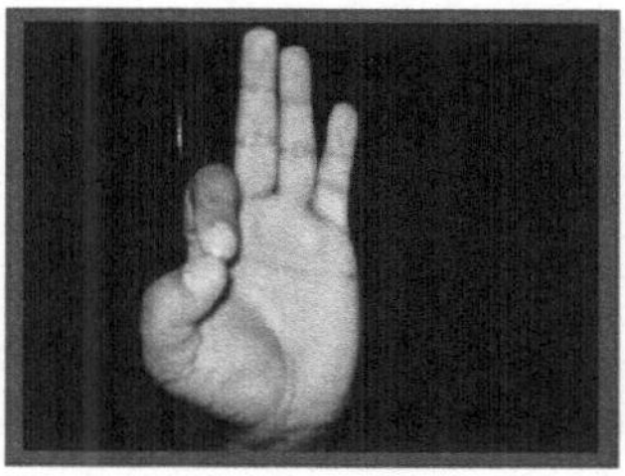

Step -3: Visualise that you are inhaling a violet colored gas slowly and deeply. Now feel violet colored showers entering through crown chakra and spreading into whole body to give a perfect relaxation to all cells and tissues of the body.

Step -4: Now exhale with "Humming Sound" and feel all black toxic gases are released. Also feel inner bliss with the humming sounds.

Step – 5: Now repeat the above steps for minimum 5 to 10 minutes. Practice slowly so that a stage is reached when one act of single breath takes one minute.

EXPERIMENT -13

MEET THE INVISIBLE DOCTOR - GASTROENTEROLOGIST

Benefits: This exercise is equivalent to jogging, which cleanses metabolic waste from the body and accelerates heart rate without requiring a great deal of exertion from the large muscle groups of the body. It strengthens your digestive system with doses of happiness and joy. It reduces weight and cures diabetes and liver problems.

Without happiness our life becomes dull and our digestive system gets affected. Therefore happiness is the way of life. Take following steps for doing joyful neurobics.

Step–1: First warm up yourself by inhaling through the right nostril and exhaling through the left. While doing so, use the thumb of the right hand for closing right nostril and ring finger for closing left nostril and also hold your left hand in "Agni mudra". While inhaling one should also visualize inhaling a golden yellow colored gas and picture it spreading inside the abdominal area. Visualize toxins getting released through left nostril. Feel the inner happiness.

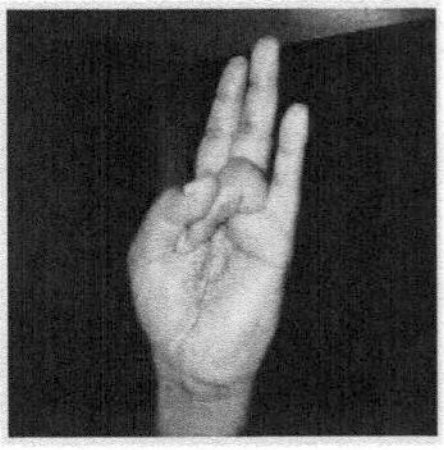

Step–2: Now breathe in slowly and deeply while visualizing golden yellow colored gas.

Step-3: Breathe out forcefully through the mouth while emptying the abdomen fully, by tightening the intestines completely (Similar to abdominal laughing like a child).

Step -4: While exhaling, feel all black toxic gases are released.

Step–5: Now repeat the above steps minimum 21 times for easy digestion. In case of diabetes, do this exercise 51 to 100 times slowly.

EXPERIMENT -14

THE MIND MEDICINE CLINIC

Remember, you will be using this room for the rest of your life and it will give you health, happiness and independence. You will not visit your doctor any longer, for minor ailments, and when you don't have to ask the medical professional for help you can hasten your own recovery.

In the present state of traditional medicine, with its endless delays and crippling costs, this is a substantial benefit.

Whatever you do, please don't skip any part of this exercise because you are going to build it with mind energy and it will become a mind medicine clinic in the energy dimension and cannot be destroyed. The power of this clinic will be extraordinary, and like any other building it is the foundation that is the most important part.

So here is the exercise:

- Sit or lie down, close your eyes and take deep breath thrice.
- When you have done this, I want you to imagine a corridor. Walk along the corridor and soon you will find a door. Your name will be there on the door and in the lock you will see a key.
- Open the door, take the key out of the lock, walk into the room, close the door and lock it from the inside.
- Now look around you. This is your mind space. You will find this room furnished with shelves and benches and two windows overlooking a garden. You will also see an easy chair there.

This is your mind medicine clinic and your task from now will be to furnish it with whatever you need.

So ask yourself what you need most at the present.

Do you get migraines? Are you a diabetic? Do you suffer from arthritis and spend a lot of your time in pain? Whatever it is, you will now take your first step towards curing it.

Let us assume you are suffering from a simple headache.

1. Sit in the easy chair, close your eyes and picture a jar. Now write 'Headache Pills' on a label and stick it on the jar. Now look inside the jar. By your simple act of labelling, headache pills would appear in it, enough to last you a lifetime.

2. So help yourself. Pick two or three of them, put them in your mouth and swallow. Place the jar on the bench. Sit quietly and slowly your headache will go.

Impossible? No . But what have you actually done?

By projecting your mind toward the problem and knowing, without any doubt that you are going to be cured. This way you release your own natural painkillers, endorphins to be precise. Your mind is controlling the action of the body.

By keeping yourself occupied you have also taken a major step towards independence. By constructing this powerful Mind Medicine Clinic you can cure all your ills. It is truly a magical room.

Visit your Mind -Medicine Clinic every day, whether you are ill or not. Add something every time you enter it. Write More labels to put on empty jars. It is much better to be prepared for any eventuality. One day, it might be a matter of great urgency.

There is no end to the list. Cotton wool, slimming pills, backache pills, hormone pills, heroin or other drugs for addicts. Yes! An addict needs a daily shot while trying to kick the habit. This way makes it a lot easier and can give the same stimulation, for whatever you believe is there in the jars, it will be there. What you are building up are energy syringes.

As another example, take the case of a diabetic. He or she walks into the Mind-Medicine clinic , locks it, takes a syringe from its sterile package in the jar or box and enough insulin from the bottle to last a day. The needle will then be injected into the skin, the skin will be gently rubbed and the syringe will be thrown away. It will disappear, incidentally- all rubbish automatically disappears. The jar or box will then be returned to its place and the bottle as well . The sufferer will now sit down quietly and relax.

A feeling of well-being will be experienced as soon as the insulin is injected. As the act of injecting stimulates the pancreas. And so the cure begins. Many people might find a spirit doctor waiting for them so they just sit down, close their eyes, and relax, while healing is takes place.

Visit your pharmacy for at least five minutes every day, whether you are well or ill. Over the months and years you will probably change things in it. Maybe you would change the benches and shelves and if you are a woman you would want prettier bottles and even some dramatic potions. With this exercise you are building energy, which is power. Its results will alter your life.

EXPERIMENT -15

NATURE'S COSMETIC TO LOOK YOUNG

Try them for a week – and see what you do for your looks and disposition!

A. Lie flat on the floor whenever you feel tired. Stretch your hands and feet as much as you can.

B. Close your eyes. You might try saying "this sun is shining overhead. The sky is blue and sparking. Nature is calm and in control of the world- and I, as the nature's child, am true to the universe. ". Or-better still –pray !

C. If you cannot lie down, because you can't spare the time, then you can achieve almost the same effect while sitting in a chair. A hard, upright chair is the best for relaxing. Sit upright in the chair, like a seated Egyptian statue, and let your hands rest on the top of your thighs with palms facing downwards.

D. Now, slowly stretch the toes- then let them relax. Stretch the muscles in your legs- and then let them relax. Do this slowly and move towards other muscles of your body and repeat the action, unless you reach the neck. Then let your head roll around heavily, as if it were a football. Keep telling your muscles to let go.

E. Calm your nerves with slow and steady breathing. Breathe from the depth of your stomach. Rhythmical breathing is the best method ever discovered for soothing the nerves.

F. Think of the wrinkles and frowns on your face, and smoothen them all . Loosen up the creases between your brows, and at the sides of your mouth. Do this twice a day, and you might never have to go to a health club for a massage.

SPORTS

EXPERIMENT -1

MENTAL MOVIE FOR SUCCESS IN SPORTS

- Sit on a straight-backed chair and keep your spine straight.
- Surrender to the force of gravity and relax your whole body. Feel the weight of your body on the chair with the feet resting on the ground.
- Focus on your breathing and include the nerve centre at the top of your head in focus. Visualize it sending messages of total relaxation throughout your body. Feel the tensions and fatigue disappearing from your system.
- Remember something that you have done best in the recent past, today, yesterday, day before that, and so on. You can go right up to three weeks in the past.
- Select one of these events and visualize it in minute details. Go to that venue mentally, identify and observe the people who were there.
- Visualize your focus and poise in the skill flow. Picture how you were focusing only on the relevant signals and how your skill was flowing naturally.
- Feel the joy of achievement you felt. Visualize the response that you got from others, especially your friends and well wishers.
- Come to the present by focusing on your breathing again. Do deep breathing from your stomach for one or two minutes.
- Visualize yourself at the venue of your next match or practice session.
- Observe yourself performing at your best with the same focus and poise as you had in the past event.
- Visualize yourself completing the event to your satisfaction, and remain in the same focus and mood for some more time.
- Visualize the natural consequences of your excellence – like winning the match, being praised and patted on the back by your coach or a well-wisher.

(Read the next experiment to know the science behind it.)

EXPERIMENT -2

THE SCIENCE OF MENTAL MOVIE

Sachin Tendulkar once said:
"Before every match, I visualize in my mind that I will get a hundred. I did so before this match too. As pre-match preparation, I do certain things and his is one of those things."

Boxing legend Mohammad Ali once said:

"The most important work was done, not in the ring, but in the armchair"

He was fighting the fight in his head while resting in the armchair.

After winning eight Olympic medals Michael Phelps was asked how did he feel on his new achievement. He said: "This is just a replay of what I have seen and felt thousands of times in my mind. I have seen this achievement like a mental movie for years."

Imagine a flawless performance: Elite athletes learn how to block out images representing doubt. If an image of difficulty pops up in their heads, they become extremely adept at changing the inner movie, quickly editing the scene to imagine success.

Winning depends on how specifically you can mentally rehearse: Seasoned athletes use vivid, highly detailed internal images and run-throughs of the entire performance. The most important aspect of the intention is to rehearse the victory, which appears to help in securing it. Successful competitors rehearse their own feelings, particularly their elation and emotional response to winning, the reactions of their parents, the medals, the post- match celebrations and the residual rewards like sponsorships etc. They imagine that the crowd is cheering for their performance alone.

Those who can combine the knowledge of the sports venue with mental rehearsal tend to be more successful than those who simply use mental rehearsals alone.

Imagining or mental rehearsal of a performance helps in improving the actual performance to a great extent.

Future performance improves because your brain already knows the route and follows the track already laid down by mental rehearsal. The brain does not distinguish between doing something specific and just thinking about doing it. Mental rehearsal lays down the tracks just as well as the physical practice does. The nerves and muscles create a pathway just as sound as the one produced by repeated practice.

Nevertheless, there are a few important differences between mental and physical practice.

1. With physical practice, when you practice too much, you become fatigued, which causes electrical interference and blockage along the tracks. With mental intention, no road blocks ever appear, no matter how much you practice in your head.
2. The neuromuscular pattern laid down with mental practice may be slightly smaller than that of physical practice. Although both types of practices create much the same muscle patterns, the imagined performances have much smaller magnitude.

EXPERIMENT -3

HOW TO CREATE A PERSONAL REFUELING ZONE

After completing "the orange experiment and various other experiments, now you know that with the power of thought you can change the bio- chemistry of the body. Using this principle you can create your personal refueling zone.

Step I – Sit comfortably, focus on your breathing and allow yourself to relax completely.

Step II- Mentally, draw a large circle in front of you in blue colour.

Step III-Inside this circle place all the qualities or inner resources that you would require to excel in the situation for which you are training.(You may visualize various words like stamina, strength, confidence, flexibility etc. are kept inside the circle in liquid form of blue colour.)

Step IV – Mentally, step ahead in the circle and visualize all the qualities coming into your system and becoming forming a part of your personality.

Step V - Mentally, step out of the circle.

Step VI -Visualize a good start and a good finish for the event and a positive response from your well-wishers.

This is a very powerful method and works wonderfully specially if done within an hour before the actual performance.

EXPERIMENT -4

TECHNIQUE OF CONFIDENCE – SELF TALK

Players spend a lot of time practicing their skills. But no effort is made to strengthen the faith that they can perform at higher levels.

How do you do this?

The habit of focusing on mistakes, failures and negative experiences has to be changed. Like the players, most of the parents and coaches also keep the mistakes in constant focus, by mentioning and discussing them frequently. They do not realize that, this results in damaging the self-image of a person and leads to further failures.

If you go on listening to a description of mistake or you keep describing your negative actions, the inner power gets a wrong message, that you want these responses to be repeated. Then you go on getting surprised at your poor show.

Both good and the bad experiences are stored in your memory and the verbal talk to yourself can trigger those experiences. By triggering the past positive experience by self talk about those moments can help you in enhancing your performance in the future.

EXPERIMENT -5

THE DIARY OF EXCELLENCE

Write the diary of excellence on loose sheets of paper and keep them in a file. It will be useful for building up a convincing self-talk.

This diary should have three parts:

- **The first part should deal with the past-** In this part, describe whatever you have done best in the past.
- **In the second part, you should keep blank loose sheets-** You are practicing regularly and also playing matches. Whenever you are happy with a particular experience, performance or when some specific thought attracts you, feel qualified to write the diary of excellence for that day.
- **In the third part, write about your goals-** State the ultimate goals of your career in unambiguous terms. Then spell out the phases and short term goals also quite clearly. Write about your commitment to these goals, the efforts you have planned and the sacrifices you are willing to make. As you write the third part, the direction in which you want to shape your future gets defined.

EXPERIMENT-6

CONCENTRATION METHOD FOR SPORTS

For the exercise,

Step I : Sit on the chair and gaze continuously at a black circle for 15 seconds without moving your eyelids.

Step II : Then consciously close and open your eyes twenty times in the normal movement of winking. Repeat this four times daily.

Step III: Slowly, increase the period of continuous gazing to 20, 25 and then to 30 seconds. There is no hurry to reach the 30-seconds time-span, and you may do it in two months time. Then slowly increase the repetitions of the 30 seconds to 10 times in a day, in another two months. Increasing the duration and time of gazing and the number of repetitions should be done only if you are quite comfortable with the earlier level.

Remember to relax your eyes by winking them for 20 times in between repetitions.

As you gaze continuously at the black circle, it starts becoming hazy and blurred.

It might also become bright and look as if rays of light are emanating from it.

Do not worry if none of these things happen.

Your task is just to gaze at the black circle continuously. Lot of thoughts will start clouding your mind when you sit for this exercise. You should try and detach yourself from all these thoughts and not encourage them. Then they will become weak and will slowly disappear, which indicates that you are making a good progress.

If the clouding of the mind by irrelevant thoughts persists, you should focus on the breathing.

This exercise will give you tremendous power of concentration on any object and the ability to keep the focus on it continuously for the required duration.

EXPERIMENT-7

BRUCE LEE'S METHOD TO ACHIEVE THE GOAL

On 9th January, 1970 Bruce Lee wrote a letter to himself entitled, 'A Secret letter to myself'. In that letter he detailed upon his wishes for the next ten years and wrote that till 1980 he would be the most popular and successful actor. He always kept that letter in his pocket. 'Enter the Dragon' was released in 1973 and he became one of the most well paid actors in Hollywood.

Hollywood still treasures this letter.

It was his way of remembering his goal, everytime he would put his hand in his pocket, the very feel of the letter would remind him of his goal.

Imaging the goal many times a day helps you in attracting those ideas, knowledge, opportunities and resources which can lead you to the goal.

EXPERIMENT -8

HOW I BROKE THE PUSH-UPS WORLD RECORD

The date was 7th April 2007 and the venue was Le-Meridian. In the presence of national print and electronic media I broke the push-ups world record by doing 198 push-ups in one minute. The previous record was of 138 push-ups in a minute by Roy Berger of Canada.

I was born with a hole in my heart and after open heart operation at the age of four doctors told my parents that, although I was cured, but I should have to avoid any physical activity involving strain on heart or any other body part. I grew as a special child with very limited physical activities during my school days. But as a mind trainer now I know that your belief has the power to change the biology of your body and the mental rehearsal of any physical skill leads to mental recurring of the neuro-system leading to the perfection in that physical skill.

So I trained myself for six months by following these 3 steps-

Step I: Physical training everyday - I used to do as many push-ups as possible. Starting from 200 push-ups a day I went up to 4000 push-ups a day.

Besides that I fixed a schedule of one hour in the morning, when I used to do about 1500-2000 push-ups (on the sixth month of the training).

After that I used to do about 1500-2000 push-ups throughout the day, at different intervals.

Step II: Positive Thinking- I had a strong belief that I am going to break the World Record. I used to think positively about the record breaking attempt throughout the day.

Step III: Mental Rehearsal - Achieving 198 push- ups in a minute means 3 to 4 push-ups in a second which seems to be practically impossible but you know everything is possible in imagination.

I visualized doing 150 to 200 push-ups a minute, many times a day. Finally I was able to match my imagination with the real performance. Often mediocre Athletes ignore the 3rd step, however it is the most favorite step of world's leading sport persons and perhaps it's because of this step they are the world leaders in their respective fields.

MIND POWER

EXPERIMENT -1

THE HUMAN ANTENNA

I am going to share one of my childhood experiences, which some of you will be able to relate to, especially those who were born in 80's or before.

My brother and I use to watch T.V. and every time there was any disturbance in the picture my brother would go to the rooftop and use to move the antenna in a random fashion, till we get a clearer picture. One day, on a whim, my brother unscrewed the antenna and placed his finger on the screw, where the cable had been. What was a mass of squiggles and static noise on the screen, a while ago, suddenly coalesced into a perfect image. We witnessed something extraordinary about human beings — Our body was acting like a television antenna, a receiver of this invisible information. He tried the same experiment with a radio substituting his finger for the antenna, and the same thing happened. He was a receiver of invisible signals in both the cases.

On many occasions it is seen that the human body works like our antenna and is able to attract electromagnetic waves. Many people who have gone through the metallic filling in their teeth claim that they are able to pick the radio broadcasts and are able to hear the sounds of the music or news that are being broadcast when they are in the proximity of a radio station.

Scientists say that under the right conditions a person's mouth can act as a receiver circuit. The metallic filling in a tooth reacts with the saliva and acts as a semiconductor, thus it can detect audio signals. Your mind also works like an antenna and has the capacity to attract ideas and knowledge.

There lies the secret of the great inventions.

EXPERIMENT-2

THE SCIENCE OF IDEAS

Einstein once said “Ideas are created by the God”. To understand this statement. Let’s consider following facts:

Fact I: The English scientist Isaac Newton and the German mathematician Gottfried W. Leibniz, working independently, both discovered calculus, the branch of mathematics that studies continuously changing quantities, at the same time.

Fact II: Thomas Alva Edison invented the electric light, in 1879, by using a carbon filament in an evacuated bulb. Actually, the English inventor Joseph Wilson Swan produced a similar electric light approximately at same time. Eventually, in 1883, Edison and Swan formed a joint company in Great Britain.

Fact III: It could have been the Gray System, rather than the Bell System- but Elisha Gray's description of his invention arrived in the U.S. Patent Office a few hours after Alexander Graham Bell's. Bell noted that “It is a strange fact that important inventions are often made almost simultaneously by different persons in different parts of the world.” (There were about 600 lawsuits over the Bell telephone patents.)

It has been noted in this history of patents and inventions, that for most of the major inventions in the world, there have been simultaneous claims from different parts of the world.

The ones who reached the patent office first are now considered the real inventors.

To understand this phenomena let's take the example of a radio. If we switch on the radio and tune it appropriately, we will hear music. Does that mean that the radio is the creator of the music? No it just receives the sound waves and converts it into a format audible to the human ears.

Similarly, when we tune our mind with a positive state and keep on thinking about one particular idea or a problem, we are able to attract the solution. But once we attract any idea or knowledge, remember any other person in another part of the world, thinking on the similar lines will also get the clue that idea.

If you have any question in your mind, the universe definitely has the answer somewhere and if you remind yourself of the question continuously the universe will definitely give the solution to it.

It might be in the form of an experience, a dream or an opportunity.

Questions exist only because they have some definite answer hidden in the universe and your mind has the power to attract that knowledge.

"Take up one idea. Make that one idea your life - think of it, dream of it, and live on that idea. Let the brain, muscles, nerves and every part of your body be full of that idea and just leave every other idea behind. This is the way to success and that's how the great spiritual giants are produced."

Swami Vivekananda

EXPERIMENT-3

THE TRIGGER METHOD FOR INSTANT CONFIDENCE

Minute One: See a mental movie of an achieved goal
Take a minute and imagine a success you had in the past.

You can use this exercise to think of any success you have experienced in the past or look forward to experiencing in the future. Remember to juice up your memories by using bright colors and big, bold and moving images!

Minute Two: The Mirror

1. Stand in front of a mirror and close your eyes.
2. Think about someone who loves you and imagine viewing yourself through their eyes.
3. When you are ready, open your eyes and look into the mirror. Now see the image, which that person would see.

Minute Three: Compliment Yourself
While looking in the mirror, use your confident internal voice to compliment yourself again and again for full one minute. If you find this difficult, it is all the more important for you.

Remember, you are changing your energy so that, you will attract more of what you want in your life.

Minute Four: Push the Confidence Switch

1. Remember a time when you've felt really confident. Revisit that time and try to picture what you saw and heard. And try to feel how you felt at that time. (If you can't remember any such time then try to imagine how much better your life

would be if you were totally confident – if you had all the power, strength and self- belief you would ever need!)

2. As you keep going through this memory, make the colors brighter and richer, the sounds louder, and the feelings stronger.
3. As you feel these good feelings, squeeze your thumb and middle finger of either hand together.
4. Still holding your thumb and finger together, think about a situation coming up in the next 24 hours, during which you would want to feel more confident. Imagine things going perfectly the way you want them to. Picture what you'll see, try to hear what you would hear and feel, how good you would feel.

This process might seem a bit strange at first, but it works.
In a moment I want you to think of a stressful experience. By the time you finish following the these instructions, your stress will disappear. It might seem like magic, but in fact it's hard science.

You would be required to really concentrate for a few mintutes, as it is important that you continue thinking about the emotion you have chosen while you go through this process and reduce the feeling into its physical equivalent by squeezing your thumb and middle finger. Next time whenever you want to feel the same confidence, just squeezing the thumb and middle finger will work like a trigger. Try to do this exercise at least once a week.

EXPERIMENT-4

TAPPING METHOD TO OVERCOME DISTURBING THOUGHTS

(Before you do this technique, read through each step so that you know what to do.)

1. Focus on what is it, that you are feeling overwhelmed about? Now, rate the stress on a scale from 1 to 10, with 1 being the lowest and 10 the highest.

This is important, because in a moment we will see how far you've reduced this stress.

You must continue to think about, what is it that was bothering you, throughout the sequence that follows?

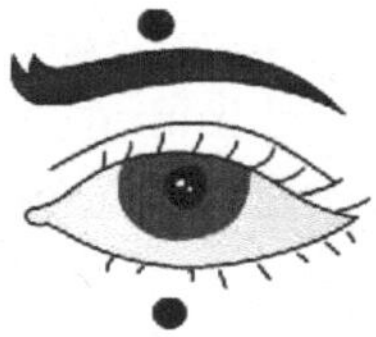

Figure -1

2. Take two fingers of either of the hands and tap about ten times above one of your eyebrows.

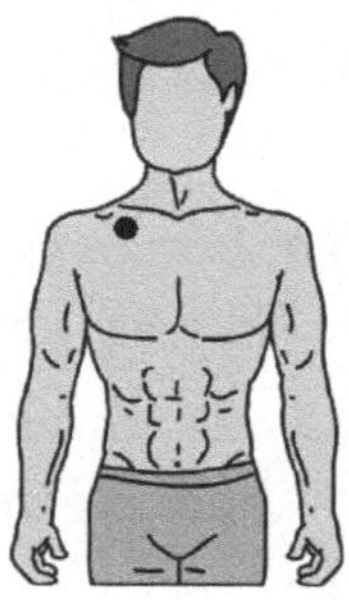

Figure -2

3. Now, tap the fingers under the same eye.

4. Tap under your collarbone.

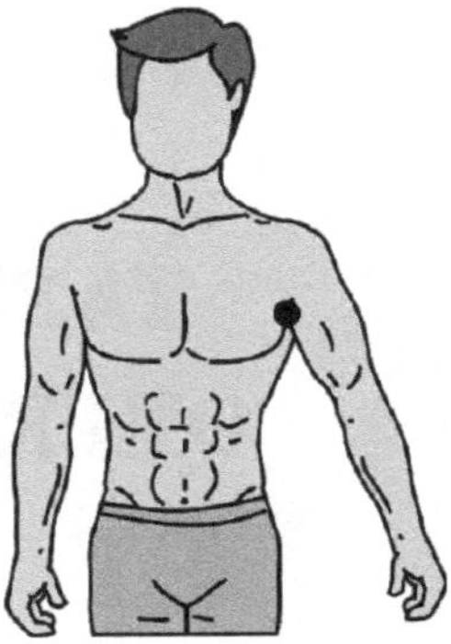

Figure -3

5. Keep thinking about what was bothering you, and tap under your armpit.

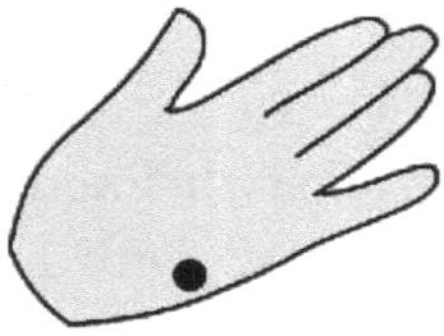

Figure -4

6. Next, tap on the 'karate chop' point on the side of your hand.

7. Place that hand in front of you and tap on the back of it at the point between the knuckles of your ring finger and your little finger. (Continue tapping that point and thinking about the stressful situation throughout step 8-13.)

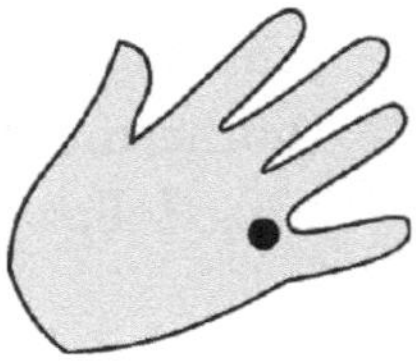

Figure -5

8. Close your eyes and then open them.

9. Look down to the right, back to centre, and then down to the left.

10. Rotate your eyes round 360 degrees clockwise, then 360 degrees anti-clockwise.

11. Still thinking about what was stressful to you and tapping, hum the first few lines of 'Happy Birthday' aloud.

12. Now count out loud from 1 to 5.

13. Now once again hum the first few lines of 'Happy Birthday' aloud.

14. Repeat steps 2 to 6. Still thinking about what was overwhelming you, tap above the eyebrow, under the eye, under your collarbone, under your armpit and on the karate chop point.

OK, let's stop and check – on a scale from 1 to 10, at what number you rate the feeling now?

If the feeling of overwhelm hasn't completely gone yet, simply go back through the entire sequence again until it goes. It may take as many as two to three times before you have completely eliminated the feeling, although most people report getting it down to a manageable level on the first or the second try.

EXPERIMENT-5

MIND POWER METHOD FOR OUTSTANDING SPEECH

Read the exercise before you do it for the first time...

1. Think of presentation you are going to make in the next few weeks. If you don't have one scheduled, think about any upcoming situation where you want to perform your best.
2. If it was entirely up to you, how would you like to feel during your presentation or performance?

Example:
Confident, passionate and happy

3. Imagine a circle on the floor of any colour. Fill it up with the feelings you desire. You can do this by thinking of a time you felt that way in the past or by using your body, as if you already feel that way now.

Example:

I fill my circle of confidence by standing in a confident posture and speaking to myself in a confident tone. I add a sense of passion by thinking about a cause I am deeply passionate about until I can feel those feelings in my body. I remember a time when I was laughing and joking with friends, and put that in the circle for your fun.

4. Step into the circle and let the feelings spread through your body. As you feel them, visualize yourself doing the thing you want to do. When the feelings start to fade, step out of the circle and 'recharge' it with those emotions, then step back in.
5. Repeat step 3 and 4 until you automatically feel the way you want to feel while imagining and / or doing the thing you want to do!

   As with any of the exercises in this book, you become what you practice. The more you practice being relaxed and confident while doing things you want to do, more relaxed and confident you become!

EXPERIMENT -6

THE THOUGHT TRAVEL

After reading the chapter "The Human Antenna" now you know that the human body has a very complex electromagnetic field and is capable of attracting electromagnetic waves.

Now let's take our understanding a step further-

The space, the air, the "Ether" between us is unseen and appears to be non-existent. And yet it is made up of the same atoms and molecules and combinations of hydrogen, oxygen, nitrogen, etc., that our bodies and other material things are made of. Because we can see our bodies, they are real, but because the molecules in the air do not register in our range of our sight, we feel that they do not "exist" and therefore the space between us appears "empty" to us.

The scientific study of biology has made discoveries to help us understand more about the "Space" we live in.

Scientists have found that thoughts are transformed into molecules called neuro-peptides. Same is true for the emotions. Emotions are the feelings we get as a result of what we believe and what we think.

Emotions are thoughts on a sensory level. This discovery explains certain mystical and supernatural phenomena. Did you ever walk into a room and got an uneasy feeling, that you've walked into the middle of a conflict? How could you sense that?

Very simple , you came in contact with one of the neuro-peptide molecules floating in "empty" space produced by one of the persons in that room.

In fact, you can "sense" anything that has happened, even in an empty room. You can sense "the trouble in the air". The molecules of trouble, anger, or whatever emotion can be intercepted and registered, even with our limited sensory capabilities. On the path to success, this information becomes very valuable.

EXPERIMENT -7

MEMORY BOOSTER EXERCISE : THE DYNAMIC NEUROBICS

This simple process of dynamic neurobics will help in improving power to recall by energizing brain cells and thus acts as memory booster.

The body has very complicated and subtle magnetic field. The right ear lobe corresponds to the left brain while the left ear lobe corresponds to the right brain.

Steps of Dynamic Neurobics: -

1. **Stand facing the east for best result:** East radiates predominantly violet pranic energy, which activates the energy centers.
2. **Activate left brain:** Gently squeeze the right ear lobe with the left thumb and left index finger with the thumb outside. When the right ear lobe is gently squeezed in this manner, it produces the necessary energy connection, which causes the left brain and pituitary gland to become energized and activated.
3. **Activate right brain:** Gently squeeze the left ear lobe with the right thumb and right index finger with the thumb outside. When the left ear lobe is squeezed in this manner, it produces the necessary energy connection, which causes the right brain and pineal gland to become energized and activated.
4. **Connect the energy channels:** In order to complete the energy wiring of the body, the tongue has to be connected to the palate.
5. **Ensure correct finger position:** The thumb must be on

the outside and the index finger must be inside while squeezing the ear lobe. This is the correct finger position. When the correct finger position is used, the pranic energy level of the brain is higher and the effect is more powerful, than if the thumb is on the inside and the index finger is on the outside.

6. **Ensure correct arm position:** The right arm must be outside, while the left arm must be inside. This is the correct arm position. This will cause the brain to be energized and activated.
7. **Connect to the divine source by visualizing deep blue (Indigo) color:** Dynamic neurobics gradually awaken the latent powers within us and also involve internal alchemy. Therefore, it is preferably safer and more effective to visualize the indigo color entering your head and spreading to each brain cell and finally to each and every organ of the body. Rays of Indigo color energize the brain and the complete nervous system.
8. **Start squatting:** Sit down, inhale while sitting down and exhale while getting up. Repeat 14 times per session.
9. **Release your fingers:** After the completion of exercise, release your fingers from your ear lobes and relax.

EXPERIMENT -8

ANGER MANAGEMENT TECHNIQUE

"As darkness is the absence of light similarly anger is the absence of peace. To dispel the darkness one has to light a candle,similarly to avoid anger one has to fill the mind with peace"

\- **Lord Shiva**

By activating power of peace, throat chakra gets opened and upper respiratory tracts are cleaned. The blood circulation is enlivened, the lungs get fully cleared, and the body experiences a feeling of warmth and peace. This exercise also helps us in getting rid of depression by making our mind healthier and resisting external influences. It helps us in getting rid of fatigue syndrome. It relaxes all cells and tissues in our body.

This exercise releases stress and anger. We can do this exercise at any time and at any place. Take following steps: -

Step - 1 Hold one's hands in "Vayu mudra" and sit down comfortably. (Vayumudra as shown in the picture below)

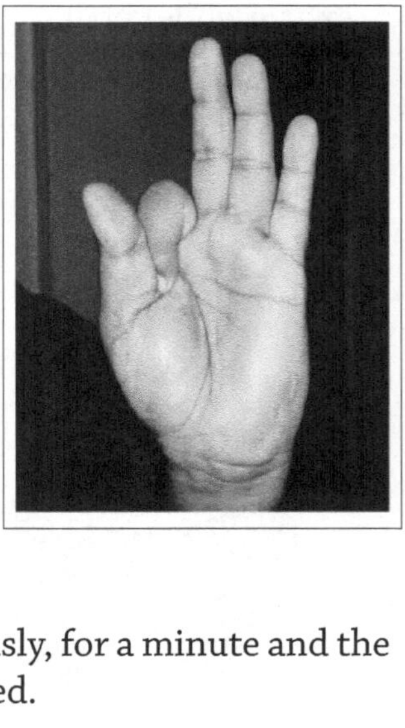

Step- 2 Take deep and slow breaths. Now visualize sky blue colored gas spreading inside your inner body.

Step - 3 Exhale slowly and visualize dark fumes (toxins) coming out of your nostrils.

Step - 4 Feel the peace within and the anger broken into pieces by power of peace.

Step– 5 Stay in this position consciously, for a minute and the dangers of anger can be avoided.

ACADEMIC

EXPERIMENT -1

YOUR OWN PHOTOGRAPHIC MEMORY

After researching for 10 years and interacting with approximately 5 lakh students, we have realized that, we all are gifted with a super memory. However rarely take any training to use the computer we are naturally gifted with.

Now, I will prove that, you can memorize 100 times faster than the current speed.

Now take a look at the following list.

1. Photo frame
2. Scooter
3. Window
4. Butter fly
5. Snake
6. Sword
7. Michael Jackson
8. Sofa
9. Gold
10. Tiger
11. Chocolate
12. Pot
13. Tube light
14. Bird
15. Key

Now, tell me how much time will you take, to memorize this list in the same, reverse and random order. Choose one of the following.

(a) 1 hour (b) 30 minutes
(c) 15 minutes (d) 15 seconds

The right answer is option (d) -15 seconds. Do you believe it?

Well! I will guide you on how you can memorize this list in 15 seconds.

There is a picture given below. Look at the picture very carefully and read the instructions given below.

Visualize the **Photo frame**, there is a **Scooter** in the photo frame and from the **Window** one **Butterfly** is coming into room, on the floor a **Snake** holding a **Sword** in its mouth, can be seen. **Michael Jackson** is afraid of this Snake and is hiding beneath the **Sofa** which is made of **Gold.** One **Tiger** is sitting on the sofa holding a **Chocolate** in his hand. He is also balancing a **Pot** on his head. In the pot there are **Tube lights** and a **Bird** is sitting on the tube light holding **Keys** in its mouth.

Now visualize the picture carefully in your mind and try to recall it.

I am sure that, you will be able to fill all the blanks correctly.

1. ------------------------------
2. ------------------------------
3. ------------------------------
4. ------------------------------
5. ------------------------------
6. ------------------------------
7. ------------------------------
8. ------------------------------
9. ------------------------------
10. ------------------------------
11. ------------------------------
12. ------------------------------
13. ------------------------------
14. ------------------------------
15. ------------------------------

EXPERIMENT -2

MEMORY CLOCK FOR REMEMBERING EVERY APPOINTMENT

In this method numbers are represented by a thing or an image and we have to ensure that the name of these things rhyme with the number. e.g.
One-Sun
Two - Shoe
Three - Tree etc.
You can then associate these things to the points in the list (sequence wise), which you need to learn.

The usual rhyming scheme is:
One rhymes with Sun
Two rhymes with Shoe
Three rhymes with Tree
Four rhymes with Door
Five rhymes with Knife
Six rhymes with Kicks
Seven rhymes with Heaven
Eight rhymes with Plate
Nine rhymes with Wine
Ten rhymes with Hen
Eleven rhymes with Lemon
Twelve rhymes with Shelve

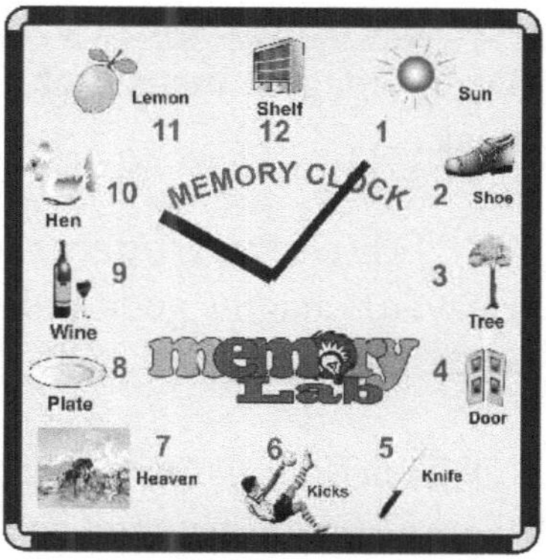

Now say we have to remember the following appointments for the day:-

3 O'Clock: Go to the birthday party
4 O'Clock: Music classes
7 O'Clock: Internet café
8 O'Clock: Go for the dance class
9 O'Clock: Taking the car for servicing
10 O'Clock: Going for the tuition
12 O'Clock: Meeting with the Chief Minister

To remember the above appointment list you simply have to associate it with the picture of corresponding time. For e.g.

3 O'Clock (Tree): Go for the birthday party
(Tree) Imagine celebrating the birthday on the tree.

4 O'Clock (Door): Music Classes
(Door) Imagine instead of a tabla you are using door to play music.

7 O'Clock(Heaven): Internet Café
(Heaven) Imagine gods and goddess are surfing the net in the heaven.

8 O'Clock (Plate): Dance Classes
(Plate) Imagine yourself dancing on a plate.

9 O'Clock (Wine): Servicing of the car
(Wine) Visualize in the service station your car is being refueled with wine instead of petrol.

10 O'Clock (Hen) : Tuition
(Hen) Imagine hen is taking tuition classes for you.

12 O'Clock (Shelve) :- Meeting the chief Minister
(Shelve) Imagine the Chief Minister sitting on a shelf during the meeting.

Or if you want to recall at what time you have to go for the dance classes, the very thought of dance will help you recall plate which will indicate the time as 8.

Now next time you need to recall what you need to do at 3 O' Clock just by focusing on the rhyming word of 3 i.e. tree and you will be able to recall the birthday party. In case you need to recall at what time you need to go for shopping the visual of shopping will help you recall the time for that.

This is usually a temporary memory and once the task or appointment is over this memory will automatically fade away.

Once you learn all the 12 rhyming codes, this method will become very handy to remember small day to day activities such as appointments, shopping lists or even important points of a speech, in case you have to deliver one.

EXPERIMENT -3

MEMORY TRUCK-I

Whenever we go for shopping we first make a list of the things we need. This list determines the size of the bag we will require.

Now onwards carry the bag but drop the list. Instead place all the items from the list in your 'Memory Truck'.

Let's say you want to buy the following:

1. School bag
2. T.V
3. Newspaper
4. Tea bags
5. Potatoes
6. Tomatoes
7. Pencil
8. Tiffin
9. Chocolate
10. Bucket

Now try to place these items mentally on the various parts of the truck.

Visualize each item vividly, in color and see it moving.

I repeat: visualize each item vividly, in color and see it moving.

Imagine –

1) The school bag is hanging on the front lights.
2) The TV is placed on the bonnet.
3) The windscreen is being cleaned with the news paper.
4) Tea is being served to the driver.
5) The potatoes placed on the roof.
6) The tomatoes are placed on the rear of the truck.
7) You have written your name on the side panel of the truck with a pencil.
8) The tiffin box is lying on the diesel tank.
9) The chocolate is in the tool box.
10) The bucket is crushed under the heavy tyres.

- Now close your eyes for a few seconds.
- Try to see the loaded truck.
- Try and recall the items in order.

1. On front light ....
2. On the bonnet ....
3. Wind screen ....
4. Driver ....
5. Roof ....
6. Rear ....
7. Side panels of the truck................
8. Diesel tank ....
9. Tool box ....
10. Tyre ....

If you were able to recall all the items, give yourself a pat! And get ready to speed away in your memory truck next time you have to go shopping.

EXPERIMENT -4

MEMORY TRUCK - II
HOME ASSIGNMENT

Using this memory truck experience you can amaze your parents.

Step I– Ask your parents to give you a list of the items for shopping.

Step II - Mentally place all the items in your 'Memory Truck'.

Step III-

- Now close your eyes for a few seconds.
- Try to see the loaded truck.
- Try and recall the items in order.

1. On front light ....
2. On the bonnet ....
3. Wind screen ....
4. Driver ....
5. Roof ....
6. Rear ....
7. Side panels of the truck ....
8. Diesel tank ....
9. Tool box ....
10. Tyre ....

EXPERIMENT -5

MENTAL ALARM CLOCK

Your mind is the most efficient alarm clock ever invented. If you wish to get up early in the morning do the following-

1. 10 minutes before going to bed sit on a chair.
2. Shut your eyes and breathe deeply.
3. Tell yourself that you will wake up early at__ O' Clock.
4. Visualize yourself getting up at the desired time feeling fresh, alert and enthusiastic.

Pursue this for at least a week to get the desired result.

EXPERIMENT-6

CHEATING METHOD FOR LONG THEORY-I

You have an exam tomorrow. You have to learn a new topic for which, unfortunately very less time is left. What can you do?

Method I: Cheating

Take a small piece of paper. Make notes, fold the paper and hide it in your pocket.

The disadvantage of this method is that you can be caught and even if you are not caught you will end up feeling guilty.

Method II: Mental Cheating

Suppose you have to learn the conditions that affect the climate of a region.

Question : Write about the conditions which affect the climate of a place in brief.

Answer: Following are the conditions that affect the climate of a place-

1. Forest area
2. Type of soil
3. Built up area
4. Distance from the sea
5. The mountains in the area
6. Direction of the winds
7. Water bodies in that area
8. Clouds
9. Type of industries

To remember the answer use the Cheating Method-

Step I: Look around you in the classroom and try to find the-

1. Door

2. Black / White board

3. Time Table

4. Switch board

5. Window

6. Teacher's chair

7. Teacher's table

8. Students

9. Fan

10. Light

11. Roof

Step II: Now place the 9 points of the answer on the above objects in a sequence.

Visualize vividly and in bright colors.

For example-

Forest – Imagine a dense forest outside the door.

Type of Soil – Imagine the white board is covered with soil.

Buildings – Imagine high rise buildings on the teacher's chair.

Distance from the sea – Imagine Sea waves on the teacher's table.

Mountains – Imagine a range of mountains outside the window.

Direction of Wind – Imagine the time table chart being blown away by the wind.

Water bodies – Imagine all the students are drinking water.

Formation of clouds – Associate clouds with the switchboard.

You put the switch on and the clouds appear, which might vanish when you switch it off.

Industrial belt – Imagine people working in the industry are feeling hot so they switch on the fan.

Now look around and recall all the 9 points of the answer and fill in the blanks:-

1. Door ....
2. White board ....
3. Time table ....
4. Switch board ....
5. Window ....
6. Teacher's chair ....
7. Teacher's table ....
8. Students ....
9. Fan ....
10. Light ....

Now, during the examination, when you just look around the classroom at the chosen objects like the blackboard, table etc, you will be able to recall the answer easily.

EXPERIMENT -7

CHEATING METHOD FOR LONG THEORY -II

Take a topic of your choice which has about 10 points. The topic you haven't learnt yet.

Now place all the points using the Cheating Method in your classroom.

Try to recall all the points and fill in the blanks-

1. Door ....
2. White board ....
3. Time table ....
4. Switch board ....
5. Window ....
6. Teacher's chair ....
7. Teacher's table ....
8. Students ....
9. Fan ....
10. Light ....

So you see, you could remember most of the points very easily.

EXPERIMENT -8

HOW TO MEMORIZE AN ENCYCLOPEDIA -I

It often happens that we face extreme difficulty in learning long winding names, scientific terms, words of a new language or currency names etc. If we have to learn a new unknown word, we have to repeat it many times. Despite this, we find it hard to memorize and tend to forget the new word altogether, after some time.

Human brain is like a huge reservoir, but still it only takes the words, when that are already there in its memory in some form or the other.

In other words, there should be a three dimensional picture related to the word, a kind of familiarity or association with the word i.e. some sort of mind picture.

But the fact is that we have to learn new, even unfamiliar words.

Now I am going to explain how you can use the technique of association and visualization to keep long difficult words safe and secure in your memory for a longer time. We are going to use the Personal Meaning

System (PMS) for this purpose. The word *Kiran* (KIRAN) reminds us of the name of a girl or the rays of the sun. It also reminds us of K.. K.. Kiran from the film 'Darr'. You remember how the hero used to utter the name of the heroine in these broken letters?

Whenever we break a word into different letters or just take a pause in between, it can change the meaning of the word completely and a new mind picture emerges.

Doesn't the word 'Kiran' make you feel, as if a key is running? Words have this remarkable characteristic. If you approach them intelligently they lend themselves to being learnt easily. We can extract a familiar mind picture out of every alien word. This method can help you memorise words much faster and you may retain them in your memory for the rest of your life.

For example:

With the help of this method you can easily remember the names of different places where minerals are found. If I say the word, 'coal', you would immediately visualize 'coal' but if I say, coal is found in 'Raniganj', you would not be able to visualize 'Raniganj' because the mind has no picture of 'Raniganj'. There are many other similar words. Let's have a look at the chart given below-

Steel	Rourkela
Cement	Katni
Brass Utensils	Muradabad

HMT Factory Pinjore

Coal Jharia

The moment we hear words like steel, cement, brass and H.M.T. factory, we immediately strike a mental note of familiarly. But when we say Rourkela, Katni, Muradabad, Pinjore and Jharia, no mind picture comes to our rescue.

With the help of the Personal Meaning System (PMS) we can easily create a mind picture of these words as well. Let us see some put two Lines here or take this Line to back page.

Coal-Raniganj

Personal Meaning System (PMS): Rani-ganj / **Rani** Mukherjee-***ganji***. Imagine that the actress Rani-Mukherjee has become bald. Yes, make a memory picture that Rani Mukherjee has gone bald. She appears totally bald on the posters of the film 'Bunty aur Bubbly'. You ask her the reason of her baldness and she says that someone burnt her hair with **coal**.

Steel-Rourkela

Personal Meaning System (PMS): Rourkela/ Rao-kela. Make a memory picture of our ex-prime minister Shri Narsimha Rao, eating a banana ***(Kela).*** You hurriedly try to tell him that the 'kela' is made of **steel** but before he is able to hear that, he has already broken all his teeth trying to eat the steel 'kela'.

Cement – Katni

Personal Meaning System (PMS): Katni/ Cut-knee. Make a mind picture that you have **cut** your **knee**. You go to the doctor for a dressing. Instead of using a bandage he plasters your knee with **cement**. Your legs have become so heavy with cement that you walk back with great difficulty.

Brass Utensils – Muradabad

Personal Meaning System (PMS) : Muradabad/ ***murdabad***. Make a mind picture that people are going in a procession, thumping at the **brass utensils** and shouting ***murdabad, murdabad!***

H.M.T.- Pinjore

Personal Meaning System (PMS) : Pinjore/ **Pin-*Jor*** (Join). Imagine that you are in a watch factory. The workers are telling one another to join pins, they are saying '**Pin-*Jor*, Pin-*Jor***' and making **watches**.

You have learnt to use the Personal Meaning System (PMS). Now if I want to know what is found in Raniganj and Muradabad, Where is cement made? I am sure you would refer to the interesting memory pictures in your mind and reply immediately.

Coal is even found in ***Jharia***. You can make a memory picture of bushes (***Jharian*** in Hindi) and imagine that you burnt all the Jharian (Bushes) with **coal** in front of your house and cleared the ground.

Use your imagination in such a way that you are able to create meaningful and familiar memory pictures of different things. Make special use of your favourite characters and situations and memorise them in a serial order.

EXPERIMENT-9

HOW TO MEMORIZE AN ENCYCLOPEDIA -II

If I ask you to think of the name of a country, say – Bulgaria. If we break this word by the Personal Meaning System (PMS), what do we get? Bull-garia, i.e. *'bull-gir gaya'* (A bull fell) . If we have to join another word 'Sofia' with it, what do we do? We break the word Sofia... into 'sofa'... and you get your memory picture – a bull has fallen on the sofa in your drawing room. Have a clear memory picture and now you can never forget that, 'Sofia is the capital of Bulgaria'.

Personal Meaning System (PMS) brings you so close to your answers that there is no further scope of confusion . Names of different countries, capitals, currency or constitution, anything can be clearly memorized by this method. Even complex chemical equations and biological terms can be easily remembered with this method. Break those words repeatedly till you get a familiar picture with a meaning. Let us have a look at some of the examples given below-

Germany / Germ-many / Many germs

Iran / I-ran / I am running

Israel / Is-reel / Coming by this rail

Japan / Ja-pan / in Hindi *Ja-Pan-la* (Go and get a pan)

Malaysia / Mala-*sia* (Stich)

Spain / S-pain / Severe pain

Sweden / Swe-den / Sweet-den / The den is sweet

Denmark / Den-mark / Mark of a den

See how we have broken these words and derived new words out of them. Now, let us try and break the names of the parliaments of these countries. For example 'Diet' is a word used for Japan's parliament. Now imagine that one of the parliamentarians is telling someone 'go-and-get-pan' *(Ja-Pan-Le-aa)* because I am 'dieting'.

Spain – Madrid

Spain / Severe pain

Madrid / Mad

Personal Meaning System (PMS) : A person is getting **mad** due to **pain**.

Germany – Bundestag

Germany / Many germs

Bundestag / Bun-*dus*-tag

Personal Meaning System (PMS) : There are **ten (*dus*) buns** in a **tag** and there are **many germs** in them.

Now let us try and remember the names of a few countries and their capitals.

Country	**Capital**
Angola	Luanda

If you break these names, what do you get? '*Aag-ka-gola*' (ball of fire) and '*Lo-anda* ' (Have an egg) Now imagine a shopkeeper hands over eggs to you and says, *"Lo-anda"* but when you hold it in your hands an '*aag-ka-gola*' comes out.

Country	**Capital**
Grenada	St. George's

Imagine that a saint has attacked President **George** (W. Bush) with a **grenade** and you are trying to save him.

Try and participate in your memory pictures i.e. you should be present on the scene as a character, as if you are talking to the characters in the picture. This will help in securing the picture in your mind. Let us take the example of another name-

Country	**Capital**
Hungary	Budapest
Hungry	*Buda*-paste

You can easily visualise a **hungry** old man ***(Buda)*** eating '**paste**'. You can easily simplify many difficult subjects in this manner. Let us take the example of some chemical reactions?

Nelson Cell **Manufacturing of NaOH**

Nelson Mandela *Nao* (Boat)

Does the word 'Nelson' strike a note of familiarity in your mind? Yes, you think of the first black president of South Africa '**Nelson Mandela'**. It is likely that some of you do not know about Nelson Mandela. There is no need to worry or panic. We can think of some other option. The mind has an unlimited capacity. It can offer endless options. In such a situation your fertile mind can make this picture – ***Nal (Tap) ka son*** or a baby tap.

With the action of Nelson cell you get NaOH.

Personal Meaning System (PMS): Create a memory picture that **Nelson** won a **boat** (NaOH – *Nao* in Hindi) competition and you are giving him a trophy.

Parkes process **Manufacturing of Ag (silver)**

Park *Aag* (Fire)

Create a mind picture that the **park** in front of your house in on **fire** (*Ag-aag*) and you are shouting for help – *Aag, Aag*, help, help. If you already known that Ag stands for **silver** then you can create another mind picture as well. Imagine that all trees, swings and benches in the park in front of your house are made of silver.

EXPERIMENT -10

HOW SHE MEMORIZED A DICTIONARY

People today recognise the importance of a good vocabulary. Many studies in recent years have shown that a solid and strong vocabulary helps you do better in school, in business and in professional life. But the common experience for many people is that the new words they learn slip out of their memories too quickly. So something else is needed beside this regular memorisation. But what?

Neerja has memorised the entire Oxford English-Hindi dictionary within six months using the same technique.

The mnemonic devices accompanying each of the words in this chapter create an association to help you remember the word. Please keep in mind that mnemonic devices used in this chapter is very much a game — an interesting game, in which there are no rigid rules, a game controlled by your common sense and imagination.

The PMS Method which we used to deal with new information in the last chapter, comes handy to memorise new words as well. In short, it is a very effective tool for vocabulary enhancement.

1.catalyst- n.—something that incites activity

CATALYST

CATTLE-LIST

2.Arid—adj. dry

arid

air-it

3. Miasma— n.—thick heavy fog

Miasma

My asthma

There lived a heavy thick fog
With his mom and snow dog.
Mom said on Christmas eve
Go outside 'my kid'.
He said 'no dear ma'
I'm suffering from my asthma.

4. Kowtow- v -to kneel and touch the forehead to the ground in an expression of deep respect

Kowtow

cow-toe

Once a cow went to his master,
Said 'I respect you for what you are'.
So she bent on her knee,
And touched his toe.
The master said 'what are you doing'?
Go go go.

5.Gossamer -n. a soft sheer gauzy fabric

GOSSAMER

go-summer

6.Hospice - n. a lodging for travellers

Hospice

hot-spice

7. Scruple -n. a doubt or hesitation in a certain situation.

SCRUPLE

ISHQ -RUPAL

ishq ho gaya rupal ko

8. Beeline - n. a direct, straight way

Beeline

bee-line

9.Dizzard- n. a foolish person

Dizzard

lizard

There was a lizard,
Who always tried hard
To look more smart.

Even after that,
He was only known
As a foolish person.

10.Gingerly- adj. careful

Gingerly

ginger

EXPERIMENT-11

HOW TO LEARN ANYTHING AND EVERYTHING

The law of association which you have learnt in previous three chapters can be extended virtually to everything.

It is all about connecting one word with the other. To associate what we have with some alternative image of the abstract words and then associate the L.H.S with the R.H.S.

Some of the places where this technique is perfectly applicable are as follows-

L.H.S.(Left Hand Side)	**R.H.S. (Right Hand Side)**
Word	Meaning
Book	Author
Date	Event
Inventor	Invention
Scientific Term	Definition
Country	Capital
Country	Currency
Telephone No.	Name
Country	Parliament
Place	Mineral
Section	Title
Minister	Port folio
Disease	Effected Areas
Summary	Full Name
City	River
Time	Subject of appointment
Question	Answer
Objective type question	Right answer

EXPERIMENT-12

SPACED LEARNING

Most students do not plan their study time well.

By taking breaks at proper intervals, one can learn a topic better.

Spaced learning should be used to plan your study time-

- Study a theoretical topic for about 40 minutes and then take a break for 10 minutes.
- Logical subjects like mathematics and science can be studied for 60 min.
- During the break you might listen to the music, go for a short walk or do some breathing exercises to relax and rejuvenate yourself.

Break acts like a pillar which holds the information learnt.

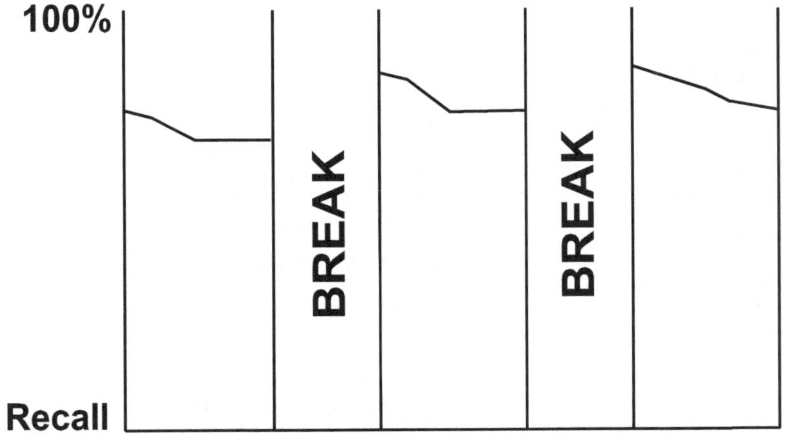

EXPERIMENT-13

LAW OF OVER LEARNING

Inspite of spending hours in learning a topic, the revision seems to take considerable time. Over learning is a way to solve this problem:

1. Learn any topic.

2. Spend one third of your original learning time in reading the same topic immediately after learning it.

Outcome:

- This saves on a lot of revision time.
- Improves your power of retention for that topic.
- Helps in quick recall during the exams.

EXPERIMENT-14

SCIENTIFIC REVISION PLAN

There are many students who study throughout the year and yet they need to learn everything all over again before the examination.

They are not able to retain what they have learnt.

Here lies the magical cure that has been scientifically proven-

Step 1–For better retention the first revision for a topic should be done within 24 hours of learning a topic.
(Because the first forgetting cycle starts at the end of 24hrs of first learning)

Step 2 – The second revision is necessary within seven days.
(After first revision the information is retained for a week and then the second forgetting cycle starts)

This will ensure a strong and sound memory and optimize chances of recalling precisely.

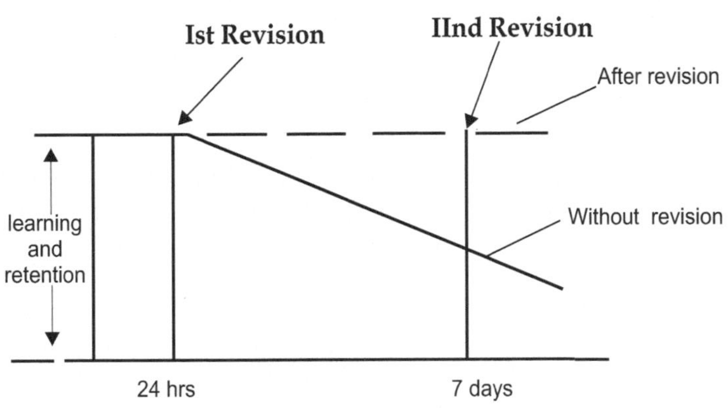

EXPERIMENT -15

LAW OF REINTEGRATION

Does your mind go blank as soon as you see the question paper? Do you find it difficult to recall answers to certain questions?

Well now you can follow the law of re-integration. Next time you fail to recall any answer in the examination hall.

Step1. Concentrate and mentally go back to the surroundings in which you had learnt it.

Step 2. Visualize yourself opening that page of the book and try to read it mentally.

Step 3. In a few seconds you will be able to recall the desired information.

EXPERIMENT -16

LAW OF INTERFERENCE

During the exams when you study for long hours you get confused because all the information gets muddled up.

You should not study one subject throughout the day.

You should

1. Divide your study time.

2. Devote each section of your time to a different subject.

3. Alternate logical and theoretical subjects, for example – History followed by Maths, Hindi followed by Science.

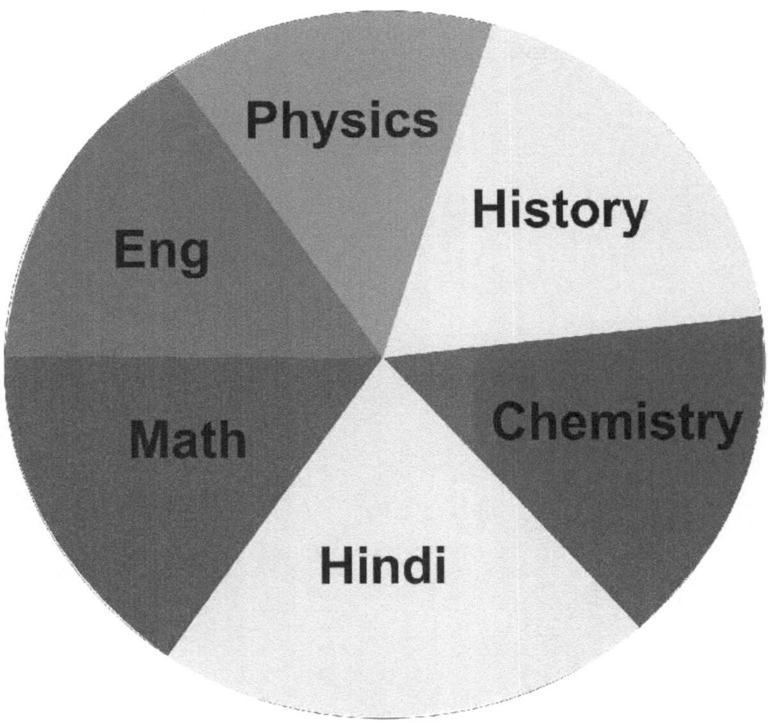

EXPERIMENT-17

HOW WATCHING MOVIES CAN BE HELPFUL IN EXAMS

This method is helpful to those who cannot stop watching films and T.V serials even during the examination days. Watching films can be helpful to you, to memorize the theory. How?

Let's take an example-
In this method you have to pick different characters and attach one complete topic or an answer to each of the character.
I am sure you must have watched the movie 3-Idiots.
Step I: Let's take one of the characters of the movie- say Farhan Qureshi (Madhvan).

Step II: Mentally run the movie and try to locate the sequence of the journey of Farhan Qureshi in the film.

Step III: Write these in points

1) Aero plane
2) Airport
3) Taxi
4) Raju Rastogi's house
5) College water tank
6) Traveling in Chatur's SUV
7) Ranchordas's house
8) Pia's wedding
9) Rancho's School
10) Sea shore gathering with Phunsuk Wangdu

Note: If any particular scene or location is repeated in the film, we will only consider the one shown the first time as in this case the traveling in Chatur's car was shown throughout the film but we will consider only the first time they took the journey.

Now let's say that you wanted to memorize the following answer.

Write in points about the characteristics of Fayol's Principle of managment

Ans:-

1) Division of labour
2) Discipline
3) Unity of command
5) Unity of direction
5) For remuneration to employees
6) Scaler Chain
7) Order
8) Initiative
9) Centralisation & Decentralisation
10) Equity

Now to memorize the above answer you just have to place the answer in the journey of Farhan Kuraishi.

1. Imagine laborers (**Division of labour**) are sitting in the aero plane.
2. Imagine that lot of **discipline** is maintained at the airport.
3. Visualize commander (**Unity of Command**) is in taxi.
4. Imagine that you are asking for the **direction** to Raju Rastogi's house.
5. Visualize fair **remuneration** is being given to the employees near the college water tank.
6. Imagine **Chatur** tied up in chains and is beaten with a scale (**scaler chain**).
7. Everybody obeys "Ranchodas's **order**".
8. Pia took the **initiative** to run away from the wedding.
9. Imagine yourself in the centre (**Centralisation & Decentralisation**) of Rancho's school.
10. Visualize **Phunsuk Wangdu** discussing about the equity of the company with Chatur on the sea shore.

Now to recall the answer you just have to run through the journey of Farhan Qureshi in your imagination and you will be reminded of all the points of the answer.

EXPERIMENT -18

LATENT LEARNING ENSURES SUCCESS

"Great athletes acknowledge that 80-90% of success in sports is due to the mental factor" (Charles Garfield- Psychologist).

This is true in every field. A positive attitude and self suggestion leads us to our goal much faster. Giving yourself a self suggestion using the mind's eye is called latent learning.

How to use Latent Learning in Exams:-

A day before your exam, take five minutes for latent learning. Do the following steps.

1. Close your eyes and visualize yourself walking towards the examination hall. Visualize finding your roll number, your seat and finally sitting down to take the exam.

2. Imagine the invigilator walking towards you, providing you the answer sheet and the question paper. Make sure you visualize everything in a bright light.

3. Mentally go through the question paper. Read the instructions and questions carefully.

4. Imagine that you have answered all the questions well and finished the paper well in time.

This method of rehearsing in the mind helps you in improving your performance, counters anxiety and builds confidence.

EXPERIMENT-19

HOW I MADE A GUINNESS WORLD RECORD IN MEMORY-I

I could memorize numbers faster than anybody else in the world and that is because of a single method called 'The Phonetic Method'. In this method digits from 0 to 9 are given alternative sound or letter. For e.g. 1 as t, 2 as n or 3 as m and so on. By remembering them you can memorise any kind of number, much faster.

Part -I		
Number	**code**	**How to remember**
0	s	0 is round as sun. So imagine first letter of sun (S) for 0
1	t	if you remove the cutting line of t, then it looks like 1
2	n	2 looks like n.
3	m	3 looks like m
4	r	r looks like *char* (4) in Hindi
5	L	L stands for 50 in Roman. Here we will show 5 with L.
6	g	6 looks like g
7	K	if you juxtapose two 7s, it looks like K
8	V	image of V would look like 8 in water.
9	p	mirror image of p looks like 9

I) Suppose you have to remember the melting point of 'Lead', which is 327^0C.

You often get confused if it was 327^0 or 237^0. Now let us convert this into letters with the help of Phonetic Method.

3	2	7		3 2 7
M	N	K		M o N K e y

If you read the letters MNK together, the word 'monkey' appears in the mind. You can forget 327^0 but you cannot forget monkey. Now we have to connect 'Lead' with 'monkey'.

Memory Picture: Imagine that you are writing with a lead pencil. A monkey snatches it and runs away.

II. You have to memorize that the atomic mass no. of 'mercury' which is 201^0.

2	0	1		2 0 1
N	S	T		N e S T

As you join all the consonants you will get a word that will automatically lead to a clear mind picture NST would lead to 'nest'.

Memory Picture: You have a mercury thermometer in your hand and you are keeping it carefully in a nest.

You might doubt the power of memory pictures.
Once my friend Rajesh asked me to come over to his house.
He told me to note down his address. I replied:
"Instead of taking a note of your address in the diary, I would write it mentally. You just tell me the address."

He told me that his house No. was 357.

Immediately I used my formula.

3	5	7		3	5	7
M	L	K		M i	L	K

MLK takes us to the word 'milk'. So his address is secure in my memory as the word 'milk'.

Memory Picture: I made a memory picture with 'MLK'. I imagined that when I reach his house and knock at the door, the door opens and I find Rajesh bathing in 'milk'.

Rajesh said, "Don't forget I live in E Block." If I had not

used my technique, probably I could have forgotten that Rajesh lived in 'E' block but I went back to my childhood alphabet books and made a mental note of E for 'elephant'.

Memory Picture: Again I created a rather funny picture in mind. I imagined that Rajesh is transformed into an elephant after drinking milk. I go and shake hands with holding his trunk.

Do you think that after this kind of visualization, you are still likely to forget?

Come, let us conduct an experiment.

Imagine the face of a friend. Assume that you have stuck an elephant's trunk on his nose with fevicol. Now what will you see when you meet him next? Obviously his 'trunk'. Whenever I meet Rajesh I tell him, 'you live in 'E' block, don't you'? He asks me how could I remember it for so long. I tell him that it was written on his face. He gets totally baffled but I know and understand the secret behind my memory. If you also make it a habit to create such memory pictures and connect people with events and use your imagination. I am sure it will be very easy for you to remember things.

III) For example: A student of C.A. has to learn section 147 that applies to publishing rights. Lets see how does this Phonetic Method helps us in remembering this-

1	4	7		1	4	7
T	R	K		T	R uc	K

TRK takes us to the word 'truck'.

Memory Picture: A publisher is screaming on the top of his voice, "Take away all my publishing rights, I have renounced everything." People load his books in a truck and take them away.

After this, whenever the word 'truck' comes to your mind, you will remember section 147.

(V) Section 222 – Transfer of judges

2	2	2
N	N	N

Memory Picture: Imaging that the judge is saying "No No No" emphatically "even if you transfer me I shall not go".

It often happens that the students of history have to learn and remember a lot of dates. This gets very irritating and uninteresting. The memory improving methods can be of big help here. These can evoke interest in an otherwise uninteresting area like this. You can make memory pictures mentally and it will make learning of dates somewhat interesting. For example:

(VI) 1919 Jallianwala Bagh massacre

The students of history have a fairly good idea about the century when a particular event took place. So we need not remember two digits pertaining to the century and we can focus on just the two digits of the year.

1	9		1		9
T	P		T	a	P

T P gives us the word 'tap'.

Memory Picture: You are in Jallianwala Bagh. There is a tap in your hand. You fix this tap on the barrel of the guns of English soldier's. Instead of bullets the guns are now throwing gentle water showers. The Indians are merrily dancing and enjoying the scene.

EXPERIMENT -20

HOW I MADE A GUINNESS WORLD RECORD IN MEMORY -II

Phonetic Method is extremely effective and result oriented. It does not take more than 2 to 3 seconds to put it to use. But at times you may come across some words and events for which you cannot create a memory picture easily. For such words we will have to devise a slightly different technique.

For example:

6- We relate 6 with 'G' but now 6 is 'J' also. As the mirror image of 6 resembles J.

8- We relate 8 with 'V' but now 8 is 'V' and 'f' both. As 8 has two loops like small f.

9- We relate 9 with 'P' but when we reverse 'P' we get 'b'. So 9 is P and b.

1- 1 is related to 't' but we can also relate it to 'd'. So 1 is t,d.

Now give yourself a test and see if you have learnt to join these digits with other consonants or not-

6 8 9 1

Let's say Now you have to memorise that Mahatma Gandhi

was born in 1869. We will use exceptional technique for it.

18	6	9	6 9
(Century)	J	P	J e eP

If we connect J with P, then first word comes to our mind is 'jeep'.

Memory Picture: Gandhiji is driving a jeep in full speed.

(VII) You have to memorise that melting point of silver is 1950^0 C.

1	9	5	0	1	9	5	0
T	B	L	S	T a	B	L	e S

TBLS remind of 'tables'.

Memory Picture: Imagine that the tables in your drawing room melted suddenly and changed into silver tables.

You must have realized by now that *Phonetic Method for Memory Improvement* is really effective and result oriented. If you memorize with the help of these methods, there will be no scope for confusion or double-mindedness. You learnt in the first example that the melting point of lead is 327^0C.

Now if I ask you what is the melting point of lead? Is it 327^0 or 237^0?

If you had memorised it just by digits, you could get confused between 327^0 or $237^{0.}$ But you have learnt it as 327^0 (MoNKeY) and not 237^0 (NaMaK) hence would be difficult to get confused between the two.

If your mother tells you to get NaMaK (Salt) from the market, you will surely not bring MoNKeY? Would you? In the same manner Phonetic Method would always make you remember that you related the melting point of lead with monkey.

21 Days Brain Rewiring Master Plan

1. HOW YOUR BRAIN WORKS

Immediately after buying a new book or a new dress, you start seeing similar ones, every where? This has always worried you. Then why didn't you see it till now?

A portion of your brain receives information and ideas that are essential for survival. If you haven't defined your goal, with clarity, you have not programmed your brain about realizing your dreams.

When you train your mind you trigger your Reticular Activating System (RAS). A part of your brain becomes like a magnet, attracting information and opportunities that will help you achieve your goals.

Learn to trip this neurological switch to transform your life.

Cue: *The Thoughts Travel*

2. FEEL YOUR GOAL EVERY MOMENT

Imagine that you have mastered and realized, what would be your major goal, a year from now. How does that make you feel about yourself and about your life? These questions are instrumental to help you in achieving your goals.

You need a 'Why' and you will find a 'How'.

Elucidate/understand your top four goals for one year and write a paragraph about your reasons, your level of commitment and the steps you need to take for achieving these goals within a year.

.

Cue: *Bruce Lee's Method to achieve any goal*

3. FAILURE LEADS TO GREATER SUCCESS

If your first attempt, achieving your goal seems impossible, should you shift ground or still persist?

You must persist.

Persistence is a valuable resource in one's personality. Being interested is not enough, you have to be committed as well. It is possible that short-term failures build your determination and insights for future success.

Evaluate your unsuccessful attempts and see what you have learnt from them. Can you initialize these insights for a greater success?

After 10,000 futile experiments done by Thomas Edison to invent a bulb, a reporter asked, "Mr. Edison, how do you feel about your failure?" Edison answered, "It's not a failure, now I am successful in knowing 10,000 ways of not inventing a bulb."

Cue: *How to be an inventor*

4. ENJOY LIVING EVERY MOMENT OF YOUR STRUGGLE

Joy and happiness cannot be ignored. You do not have to wait to achieve a major goal to enjoy life. Every moment is important, focus on now. i.e. the present. Live each day to the brim, each moment to its limit.

Your life's progress cannot be charted or evaluated by a single goal. The chosen path is more important. Identify your direction and proceed towards your goals.

Cue: *Technique of confidence –Self Talk*

5. HOW TO MOTIVATE YOURSELF WHILE ACHIEVING YOUR GOAL

Recall a goal that you have achieved, the obstacles and hurdles you faced in its way and then how you overcame them.

When you experience new wishes or dreams, do not worry about hurdles. You have been able to remove stones from your path earlier too.

The will to win, the decision to succeed, to take control and master your life must be harnessed. The first step is to identify your goals and believe that no obstacles can stop you. Strengthen yourself to achieve this goal.

Cue: *Mental Movie for Success in Sports*

6. LIFE IS A PAIN-PLEASURE GAME

How do pain and pleasure shape your destiny? We have our ways to cope with pain and transform it into pleasure. Common practices are smoking, drinking and over eating for comfort.

However, others deal with stress by learning, listening to music, going for a walk, exercising etc.

Identify your patterns for avoiding pain and inducing pleasure.

Are there some more positive ways, which would help you to move towards pleasure?

Cue: *Rubber Band Method to overcome bad habits*

7. YOUR ATTENTION PLEASE

We often avoid work by procrastination, which only adds to our troubles later on. But usually if you delay taking action, you only create more pain for yourself later on.

What are the four actions you have been putting off that need your attention today? Make a list, and then answer the following questions:

1. Why didn't I do this task? In the past, what pain did I go through while doing it?
2. Did I get any pleasure in the past by indulging in this negative pattern?
3. How will it affect me if I don't change now? How does that make me feel?
4. What pleasure will I receive by performing each of these actions right now?

We have always felt that someday we will finally be happy when we have enough money ..... When we find our ideal relationship ....when our body is perfect...when we become famous etc.

Rewards will not make you feel complete; it is the state of the mind, which will bring happiness.

We have to make ourselves happy now!

Cue: *Decision*

8. TECHNIQUE TO BE HAPPY AT ANY MOMENT

How can you make yourself happy? Can you experience pure joy, bliss ecstasy right now, this very moment?

Visualize an experience that made you completely happy.

Paint detailed picture in your mind, feel the sounds around you, put the same expression on your face, breathe the way you were breathing, feel your pulse rate and move your body just as you did then. Do you feel even, a hint of that excitement again? Is it possible that you could feel this way anytime you want?

Just shift your focus and you could feel happy now.

Any experience can be felt and perceived in number of ways. Sensations are always flowing throughout our body. Two secrets can help you experience this.

1) Shift your mental focus.
2) Visualize treasured memories.

Cue: *Science of Happiness*

9. YOUR EMOTIONS ARE LINKED WITH YOUR PHYSIOLOGY

It is very important to change one's physical state. When someone is angry or depressed, he / she often resorts to smoking, drinking and over eating. A step towards healing could be meditation, exercising, singing etc. The body posture with drooping shoulders, head hanging down could mean a low emotional frame. When we feel upbeat, our head lifts up, shoulders rise and your breathing becomes full.

By changing your postures you can change your emotions since every emotion you feel has a specific physiology attached to it.

Realize that you can expand your range of emotions just by directing your focus, and changing your physiology. Pick one of the positive emotions you'd like to feel, right now. Stand the way you'd be standing, if you were feeling that way already. Move, gesture, and speak in the tone consistent with that emotion. Enjoy the immediate change in how you feel.

Cue: *Personal museum for barking boss or a shouting teacher*

10. REMEMBER THIS WHENEVER YOU ARE WORRIED

You must have felt very angry, frustrated and swamped some time in your life.

Perhaps today you can look back at those times or even laugh at that situation.

Once again laugh at a horribly stressful situation.

Don't you suddenly feel more in control?

Cue: *Scrambling Method*

11. FOCUS------> EMOTION ----->ACTION / INTERACTION

There must be times when you expected your partner to be home at a certain time and he / she was late.

How did you feel?

Uncared or, taken for granted? Did your anxiety levels rise? Did you fear an accident? Or did you think of him or her stopping over to buy you flowers?

1. Our focus determines feelings.
2. Feelings determine actions.

Empower yourself by asking the right question.

If you constantly focus on what you fear, there is every possibility, that you will end up making your worst fears come true.

For example: You are driving fast. Suddenly your car get out of control and starts heading in a wrong direction. It might hit something/someone.

In the grip of fear you immediately start looking in that direction. The direction which, ideally, you would like to avoid.

It is a reflex action, taken under fear. Thus there is a very high possibility that you will end up slamming your car.

The reason- you didn't look in the other direction - the safer alternative.

DON'T FEAR, steer your life in the direction of your focus, away from the wall... towards the wide unending highway. Focus on what you want,rather than what you don't, and your actions will take their natural course.

Focus on what you desire and deserve.

Cue: *The science of a mental movie*

12. RIGHT QUESTION — RIGHT DECISION

One day a boy was beaten by a school bully. He got furious and decided to take revenge. In his rage he caught hold of a gun and tracked down his tormentor.

However, just before firing the gun , he asked himself.

"What will happen to me if I shoot him?" A life in jail flashed in front of his eyes. He aimed and shot a tree instead. The boy was Bo Jackson.

One shift in focus, changing pain to pleasure made the difference between a boy with no future and one who became one of the greatest sporting legends. Ask yourself the right questions. Change yourself!

Cue: *Morning power questions*

13. THE RIGHT QUESTION

Associate pleasure with change and pain with not changing now.

1. Will this emotion or behavior pattern affect me if I don't change?
2. How important is it for me to make this switch? Will I miss out on something, if I don't?
3. Let me assess my behavior pattern: emotionally, physically, financially and spiritually.
4. Does this affect my work and my relationship?

Now ask yourself:

1. How would I feel about myself when I change?
2. How would my most loved ones feel?
3. How happy would I be?

A new level of success, in any area of your life, is a new question that you have modeled from someone who's already experiencing what you desire.

Cue: *Instant happiness*

14. HOW THE RIGHT QUESTION MECHANISM WORKS

Think of a color, let's say 'green'.

Now close your eyes and try to picture green color.

Now when you open your eyes every thing in green color will

pop up in front of you.

"Seek and you shall find."

Cue: *The human Antenna*

15. PASTE THIS ON YOUR BATHROOM MIRROR

1) What am I happy with, in my life right now? What about it that makes me happy?
2) What am I excited with, in my life right now? Why is it exciting for me?
3) What have I given today? In what ways have I been a contributor?
4) What did I learn today? What new distinctions have I made?
5) How has this day enhanced the quality of my life? How can this day as an investment for my future?

Cue: *The Diary of excellence*

16. IMAGINATION MAKES THE IMPOSSIBLE POSSIBLE

Often, our brain cannot tell the difference between real experience and an intense imagination. As Einstein has said, "Imagination is more powerful than knowledge".

There are some people, who are afraid of new experiences while others are willing to try them because they had vividly imagined the desired results.

Have a goal that really excites you. Let it be a new experience. Imagine your success!

Cue: *The Orange experiment*

17. FAITH - THE KEY TO SUCCESS

Expectations enhance performance called the 'Pygmalion effect'.

In our study, some teachers were told that certain students in their classes were gifted and needed to be constantly challenged in order to excel.

The teachers complied and the students who were identified as bright or talented got better results.

However, it should be noticed that there was no study-conducted prior to this test to mark the intelligence of the two groups.

This shows the importance of beliefs.

Cue: *How I broke the push-ups world record*

18. THE CHANGE MECHANISM

How do changes happen? They happen when we change our perception and link it to our nervous system. Then an experience gets altered.

As long as drinking gives you pleasure, you will continue to consume alcohol.

It's only when you associate alcohol with dullness, road accidents, and even death, you might stop driving pleasure out of it.

Sensations of pain and pleasure are linked to our nervous system, our neuro-associations determine our behavior.

Cue: *Stress buster –Mind capsule*

19. A MOMENT IS ENOUGH

You can create a solution as quickly as you create a problem.

Whenever you have taken a very long time to change a habit, it's either because you needed a long time to change or you took long to realize that you must change.

Believe that you can change now.

Our personal and social beliefs impede change and hold us back.

People associate change with earlier failed attempts. They assure that it would be a long process and so on.

These blocks ensure that we take a long time to change.

Shake them off now, and realize that a new action will produce new results.

Though you might deny it however what usually drives our behavior is experienced reaction and not intellectual calculation.

Cue: *The Thoughts Travel*

20. MASTERING THE "CHANGE"

Have you ever observed a fly trapped in a room? It seeks an escape and keeps hitting against the nearest available window. The similar thing happens to people. They might be very motivated, but if they keep doing something that does not work, they cannot achieve their goal.

Break behavioral patterns. If you nag, catch yourself mid sentence, drop to your knees and smile. Break limited patterns in a fun way.

We program our brains and bodies to certain patterns till they become habits. We take the same exit every day and then, when we need to take a different route, we walk past it.

Our emotional and behavioral patterns are just as imagined. We are in the habit of reacting negatively, getting angry and depressed etc.

Train yourself to feel happy, excited and grateful.

Step in; change your old emotional pattern with a new one.

Cue: *Mind Stick Experiment -II*

21. PASTE THIS IN FRONT OF YOUR STUDY TABLE

1) Think of your old emotional or behavioral pattern that you associate your pain with.
2) Associate pleasure with your new pattern.
3) Is your new pattern consistent with your goals and your beliefs?
4) Keep the benefits of the new pattern. If earlier you would smoke in order to reduce stress, do you have a healthier alternative now?
5) Imagine behaving in a changed way and your old pattern gets triggered off. Can you immediately replace it?

Cue: *The Electromagnetic Field of Body*

AN APPEAL TO SCHOOL PRINCIPALS

Dear Principals,

I am sharing a story that inspired me to write this book.

The year was 1977, a four year old boy was diagnosed with a hole in his heart and at that time doctor suggested an open heart surgery. There were only 50% chances for the operation to be successful. At last the operation was successful. Doctor advised that boy not to undertake any hard work or a rigorous activity, because of a weak heart .

Just an average hard working boy scored average marks in the class and was always had a difficulty in writing and completing an essay in examination.

Now here is an another story, it is about a man whose name is registered in Guinness World Records and holds two world records. One for doing maximum push-ups i.e. 198 push-ups in 1 minute, beating a Canadian bodybuilder's record of 138 push-ups in 1 minute and another world record for memory beating Germany's Michaela Buchvaldova's memory record. He is the author of 25 books on Memory, Mind and Body including best seller books Dynamic Memory Methods and Impossible... Possible. He is the inventor of Memory Lab, Neurobic Machine, Mnemonic Pen, Happiness Machine and Animated Cosmic Energy Card (ACEC).

The most amazing part about these two stories is that it is the story of one person and that's me.

Now when somebody asks me how I could achieve those interesting feats? My answer is, by reading lot of books and getting some knowledge about the mechanism of the brain and the body.

Unfortunately those books are not the part of the curriculum in the schools or colleges.

It's only after completing all my formal education and getting rid off the burden of school/college syllabus books, I got some free time to read books of my choice. Its then I realized the true potential of the human body and brain.

Sometimes, I wish had I known these techniques during my school days, I would have spend my childhood productively, living every moment of my childhood to the fullest.

I strongly wish that these techniques should be a part of the curriculum of every school so that the students of various schools should be able to identify their true potential and realize their goals.

You can help your students and teachers by upgrading your school with mind corner (Installed in more than 100 schools nationally).

For details please SMS me your name and the name of your school at the mobile number - 09312286540, I will contact you with in 24hrs.

Together we can help a child lead a life of his/her dreams.

Thanking you,

Memorably yours

Biswaroop Roy Chowdhury

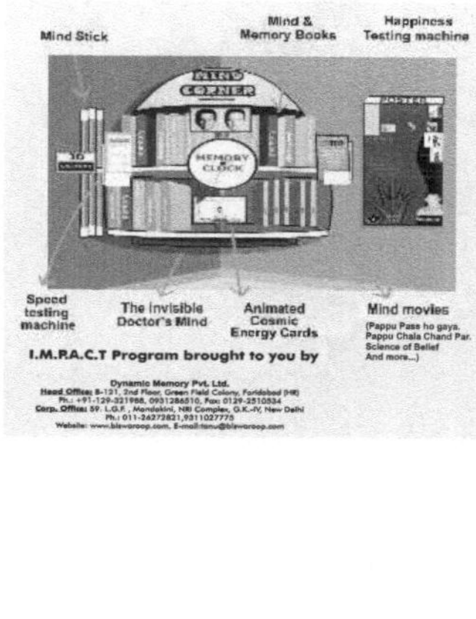

SHOWCASE YOUR UNUSUAL / SPECIAL TALENT

We all are born special and have something unique, something extra-ordinary. Think, ask yourself and discover the hidden potential in you. It may be as interesting as having a collection of the highest number of stamps in the country or as strange as ability to break most number of eggs in a minute with your left hand. Showcase your unusual talent with **'India Book of Records'**, which will open many other doors of opportunities.

Contact us at indiabookofrecord@gmail.com or call us at +91-9999436779

Or log on to www.asiabookofrecords.com

Address: B-121, 2nd Floor, Green Fields, Faridabad-121003, Haryana

Contact us for in-house workshops

Tele Fax: 0129-2510534

SMS at: 09312286540

Email: biswaroop@yahoo.com

Address :
Dynamic Memory Pvt. Ltd.
B-121, 2nd Floor, Green Fields
Faridabad-121003
Haryana (India)

To know about our products and franchisee network log on to www.biswaroop.com

To connect with me log on to :
http://www.facebook.com/pages/Biswaroop-Roy Chowdhury / 117044468312071

http://twitter.com/biswarooproy